SPIRITUAL BATTLEGROUND

THE RAGING WAR WITHIN

Now is the time to…
Make disciples to minister to those who serve.

MICHAEL BELTON

ISBN 978-1-0980-6822-6 (paperback)
ISBN 978-1-0980-6823-3 (hardcover)
ISBN 978-1-0980-6824-0 (digital)

Christian Faith Publishing, Inc.
832 Park Avenue
Meadville, PA 16335
www.christianfaithpublishing.com

Printed in the United States of America

To the brave men and women who have served this country.
For all veterans who have answered our nation's call.
For first responders who protect and serve our communities.
Thank you for your service and your sacrifice!

For the children of God

For those of you who have been called by God, it is time to answer. "Then I heard the voice of the Lord, saying, 'Whom shall I send, and who will go for Us?' Then I said, 'Here am I. Send me!'" (Isaiah 6:8 New International Version)

It is time to serve.

"Therefore, my dear brothers and sisters, stand firm. Let nothing move you. Always give yourselves fully to the work of the Lord, because you know that your labor in the Lord is not in vain" (1 Corinthians 15:58 NIV).

ServeMinistriesInc.Com

CONTENTS

INTRODUCTION

Have I not commanded you? Be strong and courageous. Do not be afraid; do not be discouraged, for the LORD your God will be with you wherever you go.

—Joshua 1:9 NIV

God is calling on you to become a mature ambassador of Christ to make other disciples. Chances are if you are reading this book, God gave you this calling. For some, He has been calling an exceptionally long time, waiting for a response. Unfortunately, many will spend a lifetime ignoring our Lord and fall short of spiritual maturity to live out their God-given purpose. You must ask yourself if that is how you want to turn out. I want to encourage you to start now. There are times in life when you come to a crossroads. You must make a choice—*Who am I supposed to be? Who am I called to be? How am I going to get there?* Some of you have been praying for wisdom, strength, and even signs. If you "truly" believe that your life has a purpose, this journey will be about you defining it, embracing it, and acting upon it. From that point, when God's will collides with your determination, you will become readied clay to be molded, to be crafted, and to be transformed into a better version of you to impact the lives of those who come across your path.

This book is meant to help Christian veterans and first responders. Are you equipped and developed to execute the mission, the God-given purpose, that He has called upon you to do? Do you even know what it is? Are you called to serve people who have also served in similar capacities? I see far too many veterans and first responders suffering. We cannot let this continue. We must reach the pivot point where we say enough is enough. I am here! Oh, Lord. I am tired of living my life day-to-day and just existing. There is more to life than my occupation and buying more stuff. There must be more to my purpose than just meeting another family obligation. I chose Your will… "Here am I. Send me" (Isaiah 6:8 NIV).

I felt led to write this book because I could not find another book to give what I was looking for. Of course, I have the Bible, but I did not have a blueprint for my purpose, my specific mission. I searched through many sources to help me develop as a disciple so I can help my fellow veterans who suffered from the effects of crisis and trauma through their war-torn careers. I was tired of seeing too many veterans end up alone, without hope, and drifting into isolation and into the shadows of despair. I became angry to hear that we are losing more veterans every day to suicide than we do to combat action. These men and women are the heroes of our country, and far too many of them end up in broken homes with lost relationships with their children. What I saw were men and women trying their best when they came home to readjust but were suffering from their experiences. I saw their frustrations mount when they could not find solutions. Some suffered significant and debilitating physical injuries. Some agonized with the psychological scars left by crisis, trauma, and moral injury. Many had compound effects that impacted the relationships with those they loved. I saw many families that had yellow ribbons tied to their trees while their loved ones were deployed and had extremely emotional and exciting homecomings that are no longer together as a family today. Many veterans are asking the question, "Where are you, God?" amid their struggles where their faith is shaken and where spiritually they have become crushed.

I see too many police officers today that are suffering from isolation, separated from the communities that they serve and live in. They are perceived as the enemy in a community that they swore to protect and serve. I see the struggles of police officers facing angry citizens due to the mistakes of a few police officers nationwide made using excessive force. Many officers have been wounded entering dangerous situations arresting criminals from the streets. They are a

911 call away from a traumatic event. They want to be there when people need them. They experience the frustrations when they do not see justice happen while trying to maintain law and order. They often feel unappreciated by those they serve. We are losing more of them as well to suicide than in the line of duty.

If you are called by God to make a difference in first responders and/or veteran's lives, it is time to act now. You must say *yes* to yourself, and you must say *yes* to God. You must be willing to be transformed (Romans 12:2). I did not want to suffer from my deployments, but I did in every possible way. I am now a 100 percent disabled veteran. I suffered physically, I suffered psychologically, I suffered socially, and I suffered spiritually. I had my whole life crumble around me like a building being demolished. I felt trapped under its debris. I cannot tell you how I survived a couple of my deployments. I do not even know how I made it through my "homecoming" to a home I could no longer relate to. Why did God still have me alive? Why am I still here? He certainly had countless circumstances for my life to be taken. People were trying to tell me it must have been for a reason. It took time for that to sink in and time for me to believe it. God had to put people into my life so I could heal. I had to have someone rescue me from the debris I was trapped under. God had to show me I needed to live. I needed to live in the memory of those who did not come home alive. I had to live in their honor. Everything that brought me to this point was based on my choices and my consciousness. I doubted and questioned what I did. There was something that God was telling me that I needed to do. He was telling me my God-given purpose is to serve those of you who have served our nation and our communities.

You must ask yourself, like I did, if you are doing everything you are supposed to be doing. Do you believe in your heart, in your mind, and in your soul that there is some divine work for you to do? I want you to know that there is; otherwise, you would not still be around. That is why I am still here. That is also why you are still here. If becoming saved was all you needed to do, God would have already brought you home. You are still breathing, so you have work to do. My work is not done. I am still growing. I am still becoming.

There is more that I must give. I have more disciples to make. There are more people who need help. I need to embrace my defeats. I need to cherish my storms. They are my testimony. There are times when everything that can go wrong will go wrong. But that is human life. The truth is, I was called long before I did anything about it. I did not have the courage to act on all the things that I should have done. I did not always boldly take the mission that God gave me to do. I did not always obey when He told me to go. I have been cheating myself and failing my Lord.

Not anymore! I now put on my full armor of God every day. I will walk through the valley of the shadow of death and smile knowing that the Lord my God is with me. It is time to pull those who serve out of the ashes of the battlefield. Help them rise to their position. We were trained that "no man or women will be left behind on the battlefield." But the battlefield still exists! It just looks different than you recognize. You may think you are no longer in Iraq or Afghanistan kicking down a door to detain a terrorist. You may think you are no longer on the police scene kicking down the door to make an arrest. But you are still at war. This war is raging from within, and it is your *spiritual battleground.*

CHAPTER 

HURTING-HEALING-HELPING

And after you have suffered a little while, the God of all grace, who has called you to his eternal glory in Christ, will himself restore, confirm, strengthen, and establish you.
—1 Peter 5:10 NIV

Be a Sentinel

You cannot be a chaplain or even in ministry unless you understand what it means to serve.

You are probably asking, "What does a Sentinel have anything to do with ministry or chaplaincy?" Biblically, a Sentinel is referred to as a watchman. As you will soon find out, I think it has a lot of conceptual and practical application. I feel that this is a story worth telling. I also believe that everybody has a story that brings them to the very brink of the point where God has them today. I think it is important to reflect on the moments of Christ being in your life, when you accepted Him, and then the precise realization that He has a greater purpose for your life. A purpose to serve others and to devote your life back to Him. It is so profound of a realization it cannot be overlooked. For me, becoming a Sentinel was that defining moment in my life that God used to put me on the path that I will be on until that time I face him when my time here on earth is done.

So what is a Sentinel, and what is it all about? Being a Sentinel never had much meaning to me in my life until I became one. The *Oxford Dictionary* describes a *Sentinel* as "being a soldier or a guard whose job it is to stand and keep watch." However, I think it is so much more than that. I see a Sentinel as someone who is a protector or a guardian over something so much larger than themselves. Someone who would sacrifice everything to preserve it. Someone who has a higher calling to keep watch and remain vigilant. Sorry, *Oxford*, but I humbly like this definition better.

To me, there is no higher calling in the military than to have the privilege of being a Sentinel at the Tomb of the Unknown Soldier. If you have seen the changing of the guards at Arlington National Cemetery, then you know what I mean. If you have not, then Google it and watch a couple of them before proceeding. It will assist in making the rest of this illustration more impactful. If it has been a while for you since you have seen a guard change, I also recommend seeing a video on it to bring back the memories of when you were there.

Now all military service to your country is honorable, exceptionally honorable. However, I am going to make an argument that being called to be a Sentinel is certainly a higher calling. I was one of those fortunate few in our nation's history who was selected to become part of the honor guard and then selected inside of the honor guard to try out for the Tomb of the Unknown Soldier.

The training, as you can imagine, was excruciating, consisting of almost nine months of intense scrutinization. It was a training process of being constantly judged on how you walk, how you articulate words, how you do your manual of arms, your posture, constant uniform inspections, and endless testing of your knowledge of Arlington National Cemetery and military history. I am certain you know what it feels like to be judged, but ask yourself if you have ever felt so judged that every aspect of your being was challenged. I had no idea how I would react to having every aspect of who I was completely criticized. However, I learned it was a process where they tore me down so they can build me back up. They were taking a young, inexperienced infantry soldier and transforming me to be a Sentinel worthy of guarding the unknown soldiers.

The physical demands were also extremely tough. Imagine being a six-foot-tall soldier who had to fit into a twenty-eight-inch waist. I remember there were many times where I was working out twice a day and watching every small thing that I would put in my mouth, trying to manage my caloric intake. My waist at one point was as little as twenty-six inches. It was incredibly challenging, very frustrating, and monopolized every waking second, all for the purpose of having what was perceived to be a perfect image in uniform to be out in front of the unknowns. Most days I was exhausted, hungry, and uncertain if I could go on.

Like the word *Sentinel*, there was another word I was introduced to that had little meaning to me at that point. I learned what a *vigil* was. I will not try to define this word but rather share with you a poem that every Sentinel must memorize:

The Vigil

In measured steps he makes in rounds.
The click of heels the only sounds.
He stands erect so straight and tall,
With pride and dedication responds to the call.
With deep affection his vigil keeps,
Over those who forever sleep.

He responds not to the visitor's stare,
Maintaining his vigil as if in silent prayer.
In the morning's twilight hours,
His watch becomes like cathedral towers.
Reaching from earth to heaven above,
A lasting tribute to one man's love.

As time and seasons come and go,
His vigil remains for all to know.
That beneath the sacred Arlington sod,
Lies three buddies KNOWN BUT TO GOD.

(Dedicated to my cousin, SSG John Gallagher, US Army Special Forces, killed in action January 5, 1968, Republic of Vietnam, and to the men who guard the Tombs of the Unknowns—JR)

As a Sentinel in training, a vigil was more than a poem; it was a solemn experience. What I mean is that we had a tradition where we participated in an event called the vigil. This was doing a changing of the guard after the cemetery closed, and you were left on the post for the entire night. It concluded with a change of the guard prior to the cemetery opening the next day. It lasted roughly twelve hours. It was your time to spend with the unknowns on guard duty, reflecting on this sacred duty and reflecting on things like the poem above. It was an excruciating notion to be out there so long. I did a total of seven vigils during my tour there. I found that time to be among the most memorable and honorable times spent, and they were times when nobody else was watching. The whole experience of being a Sentinel was an honor. Connecting to the deeper meaning of what our purpose was there is almost indescribable.

"And we prayed to our God and set a guard as a protection against them day and night" (Nehemiah 4:9 ESV).

A large part of being a Sentinel had to do with who we are honoring. We are honoring soldiers, sailors, airmen, and Marines who paid the ultimate sacrifice for their country, not only by giving their lives but also by unknowingly giving their identities as well… They are the unknowns. Sentinels live by creed, which is known as the Sentinel's Creed. Line 6 of the Sentinel's Creed states, "My standard will remain perfection." It is a standard that arguably is unachievable, but it is a standard every Sentinel strives for. This poem is also memorized word for word. The Sentinel's Creed is at the very core of who we are:

The Sentinel's Creed

My dedication to this sacred duty
is total and whole-hearted.
In the responsibility bestowed on me
never will I falter.
And with dignity and perseverance
my standard will remain perfection.
Through the years of diligence and praise
and the discomfort of the elements,
I will walk my tour in humble reverence
to the best of my ability.
It is he who commands the respect I protect,
his bravery that made us so proud.
Surrounded by well-meaning crowds by day,
alone in the thoughtful peace of night,
this soldier will in honored glory rest
under my eternal vigilance.
—Simon 1971

Facing Failure

I was recruited into 3rd Infantry Regiment, "The Old Guard," also known as the army honor guard right out of basic training. I was an infantryman going through my initial training when an Old Guard recruiter approached me and asked if I would consider joining the elite honor guard. He had already evaluated my performance in basic training, my physical fitness, and my physical characteristics. I guess I was a prime candidate for someone whom he was looking for. After contemplating whether I would take on this journey or if I wanted to become an airborne ranger, I decided to give it a shot. I remember the first time I went to the nation's capital. I felt like I was on top of the world—the history, the monuments, the heart of our American government. As a young guy, I was fascinated by everything.

I remember researching the unit, and I remember seeing a video of The United States Army Drill Team. I thought to myself, *I wonder if I can do something like that.* The first time that I saw them perform, I was completely impressed and determined that was what I wanted to be. It was very impressive to see them spinning their M14 rifles, snapping every movement, watching as the rifles were flipped into the air. The timing and the precision were so captivating that I do not think I even blinked as I watched it in awe of how amazing they were. So at that moment, I felt like I found it. That was what I was going to do until something changed.

Once I got into the Old Guard, I realized that there was another elite group inside the honor guard that was more prestigious than any of the other specialty teams that existed. I was told this is where the absolute best of the best go. I do not know if it was my ego or just a flat-out desire to want to be the best at what I do. But when I heard about it, instantly, being on the drill team did not seem as appealing. This group that I am talking, of course, is the Tomb of the Unknown Soldier. There are only approximately 1,200 soldiers individually selected in the Army to be assigned to the Old Guard, but out of that number, only about 21 became Sentinels. I remember going and seeing my very first changing of the guards. It seemed to be so perfect. Every click of the heels, every moment of their manual of arms, the sharp flawless uniform, and the solemn atmosphere of guarding a tomb that contains unknowns from World War I, World War II, and the war in Korea and in Vietnam (the Vietnam unknown years later was identified as Lt. Michael J. Blassie, USAF). From that moment, I was on a quest to be one of the best—to be a Sentinel.

I must admit, the first time I tried out for the Tomb of the Unknown Soldier, I failed. I was not ready. I did not realize the sacrifice and the work that it would take to be successful. I could not take it. The pressure was too immense. I felt I could not do anything right. I was constantly being criticized, pressured, and mentally beaten down. I cracked, and I failed. I remember that day vividly. It was a dark moment where I realized I did not have what it took. I remember swallowing my pride and telling the Sergeant of the Guard, "I quit." It was difficult to come to this point because I had never quit anything in my life. Then I found myself picking up all my equipment, my uniforms, my spit shine shoes, and lugged everything back to my car as I was about to take the journey back to my honor guard line company (Alpha Company), admitting defeat to my chain of command. It was an extremely embarrassing and humbling experience from thinking that you were one of the best to realizing that you are not.

I spent the next six months back in Alpha Company at Fort McNair, Washington, DC. I regained my former position as the guide-on bearer of the company and rose to become one of the more respected soldiers in the unit. People did not hold my failure against me. They respected the fact that I tried something that everyone knew was extremely difficult. My fellow soldiers were incredibly supportive. But I had a significant pride problem. My failure to become a Sentinel ate at me. While everybody else was looking up to me and while my leadership saw a perfectionist, I did not let soldiers see my greatest weakness. I was actually dying a little bit more inside each day. Something in my life was missing. I fell in deep depression. I was living a series of never-ending "groundhog days" going from ceremony to funeral to performance in my unit and sleeping in between while feeling completely empty inside.

Accepting Christ

What happened next can only be explained as God's intervention. I got up on a Sunday morning, got in my car, and started driving with no destination in mind. I do not remember how long I drove for before I pulled into a parking lot of a church. A little backstory here, I did not grow up in a Christian home. My parents were not believers, and I was never exposed to church or the Bible. I heard of Jesus, but that was about it. I really could not tell you anything about Him. But here I was feeling like I was in a dark, empty, and depressed moment of my life at twenty-one years old, pulling into a parking lot of a church for no explained reason.

I remember sitting in the church and standing when told to stand, sitting when told to sit. Listening to other people sing and then listening to this guy get in front of everyone and speak. I had no idea what this guy was talking about. I heard English words coming out of his mouth, but he made no sense. After getting a little frustrated and being a little bored, I was about to leave when an old man next to me pulled on my arm. He quietly asked, "What are you doing after this?"

I said, "I do not know." He then invited me to lunch. Having nothing else to do, I agreed and went.

The age gap was large. I was twenty-one, and he was probably eighty. But he invited me to his home and asked me what I thought about church. I was blatantly honest that I had no idea why I was there, did not understand what the guy was talking about, and that I doubt I would ever go back. After a short chuckle, he spent time that day talking to me and inviting me to come over weekly so he could share Bible passages with me. Honestly, I was not all that interested, but I reluctantly agreed. He was willing to feed me, and he showed interest. I guess it was enough, and I was intrigued enough to come back to his house.

The next weeks were eye-opening. He presented the gospel message to me one-on-one. I had a personal Bible study with him, and I was able to ask a thousand questions. He was old enough to be my great-grandfather, but we became friends. The studies were confusing at first, but I later realized that God was trying to reach me. I accepted Jesus as my personal savior and was baptized by my elderly friend in his backyard pool.

I found life had a purpose. I felt alive, transformed. I accepted humility over pride. I had a new understanding of service, an enlightened understanding of sacrifice, and an appreciation for how Jesus came into the world and lived His life. I studied His ministry and His journey to His obedient crucifixion. Now that is a leader, and that is an example of how to serve.

The Return

My failure at the Tomb of the Unknown Soldier turned from being a hit to my ego to something else. I went to see another changing of the guard ceremony on my day off from work. The inscription on the tomb hit me: "HERE RESTS IN HONORED GLORY AND AMERICAN SOLDIER KNOWN BUT TO GOD." The soldiers buried there are only known to Him. We could not identify them other than that they were American when they were found on the battlefield. But He knew who they were. Now I even felt I knew who God was. I looked at the idea of being a Sentinel a completely new way. This was no longer a place I could go to prove somehow that I was the best and better than everyone else. But this was a place of honor to serve. My entire thought process was different. I was now praying; I was being transformed.

> Obey your leaders and submit to them, for they are keeping watch over your souls, as those who will have to give an account. Let them do this with joy and not with groaning, for that would be of no advantage to you. (Hebrews 13:17 ESV)

The hunger to return became strong. SSG Gamble came from the Tomb of the Unknown Soldier to accept a leadership position in Alpha Company. He remembered my tryout, and we spoke about it often. He saw something in me. He began preparing me and encouraged me to return. It was no longer about self. I felt it was more about the unknowns and that God was calling me to return. SSG Gamble must have seen that in me. I felt it was something God was telling me to do as well. This time, it would be different. This time, it was about Him, about the unknowns, and about humbly serving.

> Alone and far removed from earthly care,
> The noble ruins of men lie buried here,
> You were strong men, good men,
> Endowed with youth and much the will to live,
> I hear no protest from the mute lips of the dead,
> They rest there is no more to give.
>
> An untitled poem written by Audie Murphy in
> 1948 on the wall in the tomb guard quarters

I returned to try out for the Tomb of the Unknown Soldier a second time. This time, I was ready, and I felt alive. I no longer was trying to outdo everyone else. I just wanted to be part of the team. Line 6 of the Sentinel's Creed still applied, but I did not want it just for me. I wanted it for every soldier on the team. I just wanted to serve. I wanted to be there. Accepting Christ was the defining moment; serving His way made all the difference. I felt like that was where I belonged, that was home to me, and that God was with me.

> You are the gleaming pride of the American soldier.
> Guard the unknown soldier because he is "America the beautiful"
> God bless the sentinel and we salute you all.
> ~ On the wall in the Tomb Guard quarters ~

Line 6: "My standard will remain perfection" only comes through Christ.

I became a Sentinel!

Sentinel for Christ

Being a Sentinel is a part of me. Although decades have passed since I served at the Tomb of the Unknown Soldier, I still very much consider myself a Sentinel. I learned many lessons about serving others, serving our country, and serving God. One of the biggest lessons I learned there was taking the focus off myself and placing it on others. For me, it was a gift from God. My focus was on the unknowns we were guarding and the soldiers I served with. Now it was about trying to serve whoever God placed in my path. The second biggest lesson was on compassion. I felt connected with others and began to care and show compassion, a desire to be helpful, and a joy in seeing other people succeed and, of course, coming to know Christ.

You cannot become a chaplain or even in ministry if you do not know what it means to serve. I started off this chapter with this statement. The ministry I am a part of serves those who serve (military and first responders). I do not think you can serve them if you do not know what it means to serve. I learned that at a young age, and it has stuck with me through my life. To serve is not to just participate in a service-related field and doing time. Serving is giving of yourself. Yes, it may mean giving the ultimate sacrifice. But true service does not come without compassion either. You must care about someone more than yourself.

I think a chaplain is a Sentinel for Christ, a defender of the faith, a compassionate soldier to those they serve, and someone on watch for the moment to share God in the midst of the dark times during moments of crisis and trauma. I know that there will be experienced chaplains that have served twenty-five-plus years who will read this and never considered themselves a Sentinel. But think about it conceptionally. Is this not what you do?

Each of us are "called" to have compassion and serve. Without it, we will not be successful. All of us must have God on our side. We all must recognize whether it is His will or our own desire. Serving others is His will. I assure you that serving yourself is not. If you are reading this, it is because that is God's purpose for you.

Be a "Sentinel" for Christ!

Keys to being a Sentinel for Christ

- Compassion for others is key. Compassion leads to caring. Chaplaincy is about caring.
  "Therefore, as God's chosen people, holy and dearly loved, clothe yourselves with compassion, kindness, humility, gentleness and patience" (Colossians 3:12 NIV).

- It is not a title; you must be humble so you can serve effectively.
  "Do nothing out of selfish ambition or vain conceit. Rather, in humility value others above yourselves" (Philippians 2:3 NIV).

- Remember Line 6: "My standard will remain perfection." Remember who you represent—God.
  "Do not conform to the pattern of this world but be transformed by the renewing of your mind. Then you will be able to test and approve what God's will is—his good, pleasing and perfect will" (Romans 12:2 NIV).

- It takes total commitment, a higher standard of living. Being a chaplain must be a part of you.
  "Commit to the Lord whatever you do, and he will establish your plans" (Proverbs 16:3 NIV).

- Reflect on your salvation experience and what God is calling you to do now. Do it relentlessly!
  "Reflect on what I am saying, for the Lord will give you insight into all this" (2 Timothy 2:7 NIV).

Serving the Survivors of War

As previously stated, serving at the Tomb of the Unknown Soldier was an extremely high honor. I think as a country, we do a really good job with many of the memorials we have of honoring the fallen. We celebrate Memorial Day to honor those who served and gave their life for our country. To serve in this capacity was amazing.

Jesus wants us to serve the living. He is with many of the fallen, unfortunately probably not all and maybe not even most, but many. We can and should continue to honor their bravery and sacrifice. But God wants us to serve the living. If you are taking this chaplain's course and/or reading this book, then you are called to "serve those who serve." We honor those who have served, but our focus is on serving the survivors of war. One of my favorite holidays is Veterans Day because that is the day we honor those who are survivors of their service. Many are dealing with the aftermath of their actions and what they have witnessed. This is where we come in. We need to help them with what I call the H3 cycle.

The H3 Cycle

"Hear, O Lord, and be merciful to me! O Lord, be my helper" (Psalm 30:10 NIV).

We need to help people through their Hurting (physical, psychological/emotional, social, and spiritual wounds), assisting them through the process of Healing, so they can then start Helping others by serving. I refer to it as a cycle because it does come full circle and repeat. I have heard many others refer to a similar process on a linear scale. I have not experienced this personally. The more I am around serving veterans and first responders who have experienced traumatic events, the more I reflect on my personal traumatic experiences, the more I am convinced it is cyclical.

The H3 Cycle

My experience and the experiences of those I have served and served with acknowledge a repeating pattern. For trauma, it *never* goes away. I do not mean to sound discouraging, just pointing out a reality. If you are a victim of a traumatic event, it becomes a part of you forever. You will never be the same again. I have experienced trauma before with deployments to Afghanistan and to Iraq. Those experiences I will have to deal with my entire life. Those traumatic experiences severely hurt me. I had to heal from them. Then I knew God was calling me many years later to use that to help others. However, there are times when the hurting returns, even if briefly. Then I need to go through a short period of addressing it so I can heal from it again so I can then return to helping others.

I often find that if I am ministering to others with similar traumatic experiences, I must relive my own experiences in ministry. It forces me to go through the cycle again. I found that each time, however, I can get through the hurting and the healing faster and stay in the helping phase longer. I think that is probably the best place to be. I used to pray that God would completely take the pain away from me, but He has not. I think I understand now why. It is so I can have the compassion to effectively serve those who are going through the same thing I went through. It also humbles me when I speak, so now I embrace it. I would never want to come across as some kind of expert to trauma that I somehow graduated from it, with all the answers, and then tell people this is what you need to do to get over it. No, I think God has me relive my experiences to keep me humble, have compassion, and to therefore be helpful to what others are going through. It also reminds me of my position with God, keeps me focused of my purpose, and gives me strength.

"We are afflicted in every way, but not crushed; perplexed, but not driven to despair; persecuted, but not forsaken; struck down, but not destroyed" (2 Corinthians 4:8–9 NIV).

In following chapters, you will see me refer to the H3 cycle, especially when we cover the four types of wounds. Remember it is a cycle. In other words, healing is a continuous process. This is a significant shift I am sure in the way that you probably think about ministry. We probably have all gone into ministry thinking we can help someone in time of a traumatic event to completely heal from their experience. For most of us, we can be helpful. But there is not a culminating conclusion for someone who has experienced trauma. It will always be a part of them. The goal is to help them through the cycles of hurt and healing where they can come back around so they can get back to their purpose in life to serve.

"Let us then with confidence draw near to the throne of grace, that we may receive mercy and find grace to help in time of need" (Hebrews 4:16 NIV).

Review Questions

1. What has God "called" you to do?
2. What are you doing about the "calling" you received from our Lord?
3. What was your largest failure? How is God using that in your calling?
4. What key to be a Sentinel (watchman) to Christ do you mostly relate to?
5. The H3 cycle consists of __________, __________, and ___________.
6. True/False: Someone who experiences a traumatic event ultimately can fully be healed from it? Why or why not?
7. Have you experienced trauma before? Was this news to you that you may relive your traumatic experiences when ministering to others with a similar experience that will make you go through the H3 cycle as well?

CHAPTER 2

TYPES OF WOUNDS

Heal me, O Lord, and I shall be healed; save me, and I shall be saved, for you are my praise.

—Jeremiah 17:14

Understanding How We Are Wounded

IN MINISTRY, ONE OF THE greatest needs is helping someone with their wounds. We often want to directly point them to Jesus, pray for them, and we call this ministry. I am going to make an argument that suggests that although this is not wrong, it is not enough. I am not to suggest that Jesus is not enough, because He is. I am suggesting that we are to help someone in their time of need when they are wounded so they can see God in His glory in their lives. There are many biblical examples of this where Jesus would perform a healing miracle before He gave a message or made a point of who He was.

In each instance, Jesus healed a wound in order that His message would be received. Sometimes, that message was about sin, and other times, it was about who He was. But He addressed the ailment that the person was suffering from. In today's day and age, I have not met a person capable of healing someone instantly like Jesus did. The Bible also shows how Jesus's disciples were capable of healing others. But I have not seen anyone with that power today. What I do see is modern medicine and technology. After closely looking at the present circumstances, this is what I discovered. God is the ultimate healer of any condition. God has granted us modern technology and modern medicine. He has given doctors the knowledge to care for people even if they do not recognize that knowledge comes from God. People heal through God's healing process He designed in the human body. Yet medical miracles still happen every day through the power of prayer. But wait! I stated that pointing people to Jesus and prayer was not enough, right? The main reason is that people struggle with understanding either why this medical issue has happened to them or why they must suffer. In both instances, they are questioning God. Therefore, they are stuck with the notion of prayer, and they become angry with God and question if God is even there or even cares. This is the value of you being in ministry! We must meet their immediate ailment and then show them that God still loves them.

Types of Wounds

In chapter 1, I addressed *h*urting as one of the components of the H3 cycle. Obviously, this is about hurting from wounds. In a short review, we need to help people through their *h*urting (physical, psychological/emotional, social, and spiritual wounds), assisting them through the process of *h*ealing so they can then start *h*elping others by serving. Let's look at hurting in more detail by looking at the types of wounds:

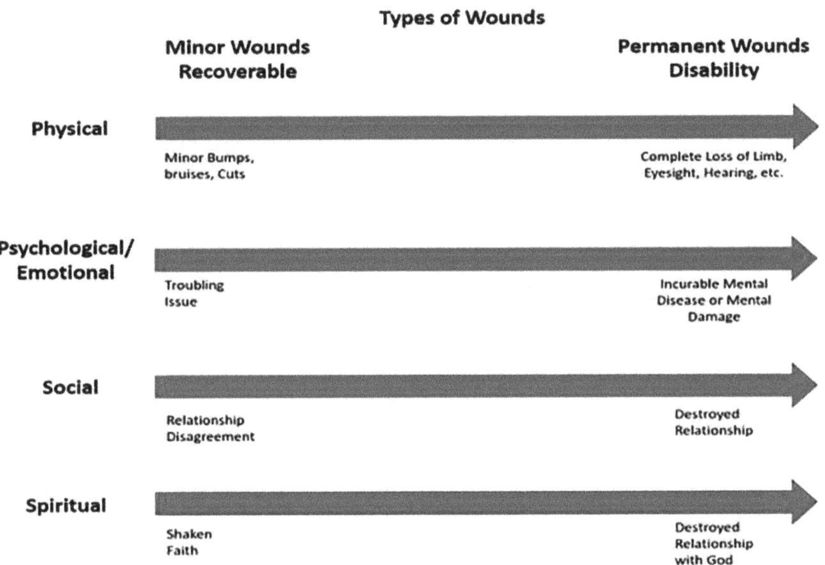

To help further explain the types of wounds and the impacts on us, we need to realize that we all get wounded in life, and we all get wounded in each of these areas, some more significantly than others. Some wounds we can treat ourselves and will heal from in time. Some may leave scars. Some may require professional medical attention. Yet others may be so damaging that a person will never completely recover from the damage. Let us look at this in greater detail. The information below will help you assess those who are suffering and how you can help. Some points are obvious, but some are not. There are certain presuppositions we all have. Do not skip this portion because there are points here you need for effective ministry.

Physical

"Be gracious to me, O Lord, for I am languishing; heal me, O Lord, for my bones are troubled" (Psalm 6:2 NIV).

Starting off with physical wounds is the easiest topic for us all to relate to. A wound can be as simple as a minor cut, bruise, or bump that you can treat yourself, or you can just let your body heal from it. It is an annoyance but does not really impact your lifestyle.

We have all had them. Obviously, broken bones, ligament tears, and organ issues, especially if they require surgery, are even more impactful on us. Cancer is another area that impacts us even more severely. However, loss of a limb, loss of eyesight, loss of a bodily function, terminal cancer, and any other irreversible wound are life changing. I am sure you are thinking through this as you are reading this. The more you think about it, the more you realize that there are different ways to help others during these circumstances when you come across them in ministry.

For those who serve (military and first responders), physical wounds are going to happen and happen regularly. Having served in the Army for almost twenty-seven years, there was always someone in my unit who was dealing with an injury. I dealt with many personally. As a commander, I remember looking at those situations with a focus on readiness. I had to assess how bad the injury was. Were they hurt, or were they injured? There is a difference. Could the soldier still do their mission? Did I have to get them medevaced? Would they be on a duty profile? Would they need to be replaced? How long would they be out of commission? Would they be a permanent loss to me? As you can tell, I had to assess where they were on the spectrum and the impacts on the greater picture—our unit's mission.

We too are concerned about readiness (shocking, right?), but in ministry, we have a different readiness focus. It is not on unit mission readiness as much as it is on life mission readiness. Now I know this is a new concept for many. I have met many in ministry that have either lost sight of this or never made the realization in the first place. So let us discuss this. Remember back to the H3 cycle. As chaplains, we are helping their hurts so they can heal. For what purpose? So they can help others. It is still about readiness. Sometimes, in ministry, we lose sight that the one we are ministering to has a God-given purpose. We are supposed to help them get back to doing it by ministering to all their obstacles that are presently preventing them from doing so.

Assessing their "need" is your job in ministry. I often counsel those who serve in ministry about doing more than just talking and praying for someone. You certainly can be there and talk with them, and you certainly should pray for them. Praying for their healing is extremely important as all healing comes from God. But often we need to do more as chaplains. You may realize that they need to see a doctor. You may even need to encourage them to go to the hospital or make an appointment. You may even need to take them there. In other situations, you may need to call 911 to get an ambulance to them. Chaplains can even serve in natural disaster situations and can find themselves administering first aid and CPR, providing basic comfort, and contacting emergency services. On that note...

Be sure you stay current on basic first aid and CPR certifications!

For more debilitating wounds, you may need to assist them by pointing them to services in their area or to national-level organizations. Again, you may even need to take them or place the call for them. I find it especially important to know about the services in my area from local all the way to national-level services. They include other ministries, church resources, corporations, veterans' organizations, veterans' hospitals, and health services. We will talk more about this in the final chapter of this book. Our ministry actively seeks these organizations out, so we have this information for our chaplains. The focus on ministry is meeting the "initial need" and putting them on a path where they can be self-sustaining. This includes you being there, talking, and praying with them. But you need to focus on readiness. Once they are self-sustaining, they need to also be encouraged to get back to their God-given purpose.

Psychological/Emotional

Unlike physical wounds, psychological and emotional wounds are far more complex. This is an area that a chaplain must navigate with caution. Our intent is to be helpful, but we can also do more damage than good. Most people I have worked with in ministry approach this area with listening and then referring them to professional help. This is not a wrong approach, but let us discuss this further.

Oxford Dictionary definitions:
Psychological: *Oxford* defines this as "of, affecting, or arising in the mind; related to the mental and emotional state of a person."
Emotional: *Oxford* defines this as "relating to a person's emotions."

You can see why these two are put in the same category of wounds. They are very closely related. But I would like to propose a subtle difference. Psychological is when something happens that impacts your mind or brain matter. Emotional is how you feel about it. It is a subtle difference but not significant enough to separate them into different types of wound.

For those who serve, we are faced with the issue of Post-Traumatic Stress Disorder (PTSD). Many years of war created a lot of veterans with this condition. I think as chaplains, we can safely determine when someone is dealing with Post-Traumatic Stress, but the "disorder" is something that must be left to a psychologist diagnosis. As chaplains, we could be the "first responder" to someone who has experience a traumatic event. I have seen this a lot in combat: soldiers losing a close friend in combat, a witness of an IED that leaves a battle buddy killed or dismembered, the realization that you pulled a trigger that killed someone, seeing mass destruction and dead bodies, etc. Not only have I seen the shock that others experience, but I have also dealt with it myself (I am even still dealing with it on my H3 cycle).

On the spectrum within the graph, I show a psychological, emotional wound as being troubling on one end of the scale to an event that can cause permanent psychological damage on the other. It is hard to determine after a traumatic event if it caused permanent damage to the person because everyone is a little different. I have seen people in such a state of "shock" that they cannot comprehend or even function but later appeared to deal with it simply fine. I have seen others who appear normal at first, but the effects appear more damaging later after a period of reflection sets in. I think we can both agree that a professional psychologist needs to determine the severity of damage.

It is important to note, trauma needs to be treated. Suppressing trauma can lead to longer damaging effects. This is certainly the case for psychological/emotional wounds. I see veterans who are dealing with many residual effects from not dealing with the trauma they experience, which has second- and third-order effects. It leads to loss of a marriage, loss of child custody, and sometimes visitation rights, imprisonment, loss of employment, homelessness, and more. For first responders, all the same residual effects can happen. The trauma itself or in combination of the residual effects even leads to suicide. You may be one of the few, maybe the only one, in contact with the veteran or first responder who can help them. In each case, I am a proponent of staying engaged as their chaplain (most of all as a friend), getting them help, and staying engaged with them while they are going through treatment. This is a long-term ministry investment.

Personalize your ministry. I know it opens you up to wounds as well. But people do not want to be ministered to. They want a friend they can trust. You need to be both a friend and a minister. But most of all, they need to know you care. People are very perceptive. Ask yourself how perceptive you are. Can you not tell when someone is genuinely being real with you? Can you tell when someone really cares? Of course, you can. Everyone else can too!

Social

Social wounds are caused by relationships. God has designed us to be relational creatures to potentially have a relationship with him and to have relationships with other people. Relationships are also one of the leading causes of wounds. We simply do not live by the "golden rule" and treat others the way we want to be treated. If we did, imagine how much better the world would be. Everyone would be our friends, no war, no divorce, no feelings of being hurt, no pain, no tears...almost sounds like heaven, right?

Unfortunately, for now, we are not in heaven, and we have all been wounded by relationships. A very troubling thought is that we have all hurt other people in relationships. Yes, you are part of the problem too. It is universal! But some social wounds can be extremely damaging. The model above shows that on one side of the scale, we can be wounded by a simple argument. Some we blow off after a little frustration; others can linger. But failed relationships can cause permanent damage. An example of this is divorce, especially with children involved. The children involved are wounded too. The couple and the children will never be the same again, and they were all permanently damaged from the situation. When either party moves on, they carry that "baggage" with them, and it will affect their next relationship. The permanent damage of that wound is still there, and it changed them.

A common crisis is where you lose a loved one. This is also a social wound. Everyone who lives a while will experience this type of social wound in life. It is part of the "circle of life," but loss can also happen unexpectedly. If that person was part of your support emotionally, financially, or otherwise, you are wounded. It will take time to heal if you ever fully heal at all.

Wounds can also happen within a social group setting. You can have an embarrassing moment, an altercation that places you in exile of that group, a change in social status where you no longer fit in, or any other circumstance where you were once part of the group but now you are not. What if that group was part of your identity? Being removed from it may feel like a significant loss. People in the military and first responders feel a social effect that deeply impacts them when they separate from service.

When I left the Army after twenty-seven years, it was not under my own terms. I thought I was tracking for promotion. Suddenly, I was starting to have medical issues. Naturally, they took my blood and noticed irregularities. The hospital sent my lab work to a specialty clinic. The results came back weeks later, and I was diagnosed with leukemia. This was automatic grounds for a Medical Evaluation Board (MEB) where the MEB determined that I was "undeployable" and "unfit for active duty service." Long story short, I was declared

100 percent disabled, and regulations stated that I must be removed from active duty service within ninety days of notification. You can imagine the shock this was to me and my family. I was not sure how serious my health condition (my cancer) was, and I was having my career taken away from me simultaneously. My world was falling apart.

I counsel those separating from the military all the time. Most deal with an identity crisis when they separate even if they voluntarily separated or retired. It still is a major adjustment, but I think it is worse for those who are involuntarily separated because they are wounded. The "system" took something from them and destroyed their social environment. The experience damaged who they were in that environment, and the change means redefining in many cases who you are. We will cover this more in a later chapter. But for now, recognize that this is a common social wound you will face in ministry.

People bailing on you in relationships or you bailing on them, fighting and no longer speaking to someone or someone not speaking to you, not forgiving someone or someone not forgiving you, and the list can go on are wound causing. Permanent damage comes in when it destroys the relationship and, more importantly, your view of relationships. Some may argue that this is in the emotional/psychological category, and in most cases, it is as well. We will cover that more when we talk about compounding effects/wounds. Remember social wounds are a separate type of wound because these wounds are directly relationship based.

Spiritual

A spiritual wound is not one that we either acknowledge or, in most cases, recognize. It is therefore the most complex to understand and identify. In the model, it may be as minor as an incident that shakes your faith. It could be a comment someone made, information that you were presented, or an incident that happens that makes you question God. In the most minor of cases, your faith is not significantly challenged, but you question it. When your faith is shaken as a Christian, it is a wound. You will probably get past it relatively quickly and recover, but you certainly do not want your faith shaken often. As Christians, we always want our faith to remain intact. When it does not, when we are wounded, we must heal from it like any other wound before we feel our faith is strong again.

This type of wound can sound a lot like a social wound because it is predominately based on our relationship with God. But it is separate. Think of social wounds more about your human interactions. When you think spiritual wounds, think more about your interaction/relationship with God. The issue is that we think sometimes that God is wounding us. However, it is something or someone else doing the wounding, but we place the blame on God. We see it either through the lens that somehow God is responsible and has wounded us, or God has allowed us to be wounded. That is why this is extraordinarily complex. Our illogical rationale leads us to misunderstand the real cause.

We tend to misdirect issues in the physical realm by allowing them to damage our spiritual place/relationship with God. An example of this is when you lose trust or have been hurt by a pastor and you stop going to church, you stop praying, and you no longer believe in God. Sounds extreme, but it happens all the time. I cannot tell you the countless number of people I have spoken to about God and that they do not believe because of some bad experience that happened to them. They end up blaming God and not the real cause for the wound—in this example, the pastor. I often say the biggest stumbling block to a strong relationship with God is man. Many people do not go to church and do not accept Jesus because of all the bad things that they have either heard or have seen occur in churches. There are millions of stories about people representing God doing horrible acts. What people fail to see is that this is man and not God making those mistakes.

I have even heard people tell me, "Why do you want to be a Christian? Christians are some of the meanest people I know." Again, this person was wounded by "Christians" who have impacted them from having a relationship with God. Who is to blame for this?

Obviously, it is the people who did not treat this person right, not God.

The most damaging of these wounds is a destroyed relationship with God. This includes those who never had a relationship with God in the first place. The relationship may have been destroyed before it even began because of other people. But God wants a relationship with everyone. He is right there, everywhere, all the time. God is not in the business of destroying a relationship with anyone, even Lucifer who fell from heaven. Yes, it was God who cast him out, but it was Lucifer that destroyed the relationship. For a third of the angels that fell, it was a conscious decision of each angel who chose Lucifer over God. I have met people who are so damaged spiritually that I categorize it as a permanent wound. I genuinely believe it will take a miracle from God to heal them.

Compounding Effects

"The Lord sustains him on his sickbed; in his illness you restore him to full health" (Psalm 41:3).

Compounding effects is an important component to talking about wounds. While you were reading through each other the explanations of the wounds. More than once, you probably felt that one bled over to another type of wound, that there are instances when they are blended. That is because they are all connected. This sounds even more complex, doesn't it? Well, it is. I want to take you through a difficult, all too real, illustration to make this point.

Case study. Jason was a soldier serving in Iraq. He went on a convoy for a resupply mission and was hit by an IED. He loses his left leg and suffers from a major concussion, leaving him unconscious. He is evacuated from the battlefield remaining completely unconscious and wakes up in a military hospital in Landstuhl, Germany, several days later. He has no idea where he is at. Then the horror sets in when he is told about what happened and where he is at, and he looks down and sees his left leg missing. He is permanently dismembered, and although the remaining part of his limb will heal, he will never get his leg back. He is permanently physically wounded.

The loss of his leg has a huge psychological/emotional impact on Jason. He is also suffering from a Traumatic Brain Injury (TBI) from the blast. He is having nightmares of the last mission replaying in his mind, suffering from Post-Traumatic Stress Disorder (PTSD), having serious issues accepting that his life has forever changed with the loss of his leg, and his emotions are all over the place. You can see that the TBI was a physical wound, but the other wounds are more psychological/emotional. However, they are caused by the same event and the realization of the physical wounds.

After several months, Jason begins to heal enough to return home and gets reunited with family. Still suffering from the psychological/emotional effects of what happened to him, it starts impacting his relationships with his family. His family is initially supportive and sees Jason as a true American hero. However, the mood changes as Jason's issues become unbearable for those around him. His wife leaves him and takes the children with her. She sees him as "crazy" and even a danger to the family. Jason becomes angry and violent. This also impacts every relationship Jason and his wife had. Socially, people see Jason as someone who is screwed up from the war and someone who needs serious help. But their reaction is to start distancing themselves from Jason. Jason is later placed through a Medical Evaluation Board (MEB) and separated from the military on a disability retirement. Even his buddies in the military stop coming around after a while.

Jason is alone now. He cries out to God in anger, "Why? Why? Why? Why did you allow this to happen to me? I was serving you, my country, and my family. All of you have left me, and now I am a cripple. Where were you, and where are you now?" Jason takes to drinking and starts "spiraling into a very dark place" where he no longer wants to live. He screams out to God, "I HATE YOU!" as he places his 9-mm Beretta to the temple of his forehead.

Pretty dismal story, isn't it? Unfortunately, it is more common than anyone wants to realize or admit. All wounds have compounding effects. If you are severely physically wounded, it will have an impact on you psychologically/emotionally, socially, and spiritually. Mix it up any way you want to, and you will see that if you are severely impacted by one type of wound, it will have a bleed-over effect into other types of wounds. Some have questioned this principle when it comes to the spiritual component. But think about it, if your relationship gets destroyed with God, it will affect your relationships with others. It will impact you psychologically and emotionally. All this will start impacting your health physically.

Let us get back to the case of Jason. Do you see a place for a chaplain in his life? Certainly, preblast of the IED, you would hope a chaplain was talking to him. You would hope he had a great pastor at his home church. You would hope that he already accepted Jesus Christ as his Lord and savior. What if I told you all this was true about Jason? How about postblast? It should be obvious from the time he woke up in the hospital until that dark moment that he put a gun to his head that he needed someone talking to him. In Jason's case, he did not have a chaplain there. He never went back to his home church either because he did not want anyone to feel sorry for him, and he did not reach out for any help. This too is all too common.

Application

"Behold, I will bring to it health and healing, and I will heal them and reveal to them abundance of prosperity and security" (Jeremiah 33:6).

When we assess people and their wounds, we need to realize that they do not fit nicely into any one category or type of wound. They bleed over. In ministry, that is why I say you must do more than point people to Jesus and pray for them. You need to do that, plus more, a lot more. Like Jesus, you must be willing to help them with their needs physically, psychologically/emotionally, and socially so that that you can reach them spiritually. Jesus's message was received by many because of the healing miracles He performed as mentioned at the beginning of this chapter. When Jesus met their immediate need, they paid attention to what he had to say.

Now let us get serious here.

Any chaplain or pastor who tries to reach someone like Jason by pointing them to Jesus and praying for them *will not reach him*! Mainly because they do not understand what Jason is going through and that he is already spiritually wounded. Jason was bleeding from all the types of wounds. That includes spiritual wounds. This is a common mistake that happens all the time. That is why people who suffer from trauma are not being reached.

To reach Jason as a chaplain, you must invest in him. The greatest investment you can give is your time. You must aggressively go to him and be around him. That means being by his side. Whenever along the path of the recovery you enter, there you must remain with him while he goes through the H3 cycle. This may mean visiting him through surgeries, hospital appointments, house visits, lunches, and any other time you can get around him. You both need to become friends. Also, you must be stronger than the situation. He may direct a lot of the anger at you because you are there. That is where your relationship with Christ must be stronger than that relationship with Jason. You will have storms to weather with Jason, and you must be the connection to Christ so you can pull him through the storm.

The solution is not just visiting Jason in the hospital to pray for him and ask him if he needs anything. This is what I see most chaplains/pastors do. That is not effective ministry. Jason will not connect with your prayer, and he will tell you he does not need anything. You have done nothing! You need to take the journey with him in good times and bad. You need to invest in him. Understanding the H3 cycle and the types of wounds will help prepare you for this mission. The chapters that come will equip you to truly reach a guy like Jason who suffered real trauma to really get to a place where Jesus works in his life. That is God's calling on your life.

Review/Application Questions

1. The four types of wounds are __________, ___________, ______________, and ___________.
2. T/F: All types of wounds can be anywhere from minor to debilitating.
3. A chaplain should be sure to stay current on ________, _______, ______, and ______ certifications.
4. Do you think you should personalize your ministry? What do you think the effects would be?
5. What do you think you can do to help someone transition from service?
6. List five things you would have done to help Jason.
7. What is the greatest investment in ministry?

CHAPTER 

COMPLEXITY OF TRAUMA

Fear not, for I am with you; be not dismayed, for I am your God; I will strengthen you, I will help you, I will uphold you with my righteous right hand.

—Isaiah 41:10

When most people come into ministry, they come into it with some of the following common experiences: seminary graduate, other college degrees, life experience, work experience, church experience, small group experience, etc. Maybe they led church committees, small groups, ministries, and more in the church. However, none of these experiences prepared them or prepares you to deal with trauma. To me, working with someone who has experienced trauma is probably the single largest issue you could face in ministry. Mainly because we really do not know what to say or to do. If we have not experienced a similar traumatic experience, we really cannot relate. I have even seen professional psychologists, pastors, and doctors struggle in this area. The only way we can examine this further is for me to give you an illustration to make various points on dealing with trauma more applicable to you.

I strive hard not to make this book about me, but my personal examples sometimes are the best illustrations to make a point that I know. That being stated, the illustrations I say about me are nothing I am proud of. They often show my weakness and vulnerabilities. But I believe, God is using these experiences to help others. Being transparent to explain the situation is important. So I am more than willing to share for the purposes of greater understanding. Most of what you are about to read is very troubling to me. It will be hard for me to write, to share, and to use to make illustrative points. I hope this will help you in ministry.

Initial Invasion of Iraq in 2003

I want to start talking about trauma explaining the most traumatic part of my life. It was the initial invasion into Iraq in 2003 as part of the 3rd Infantry Division. I was the logistics company commander of A/203rd Forward Support Battalion (FSB), 3rd Brigade Combat Team (BCT)-(Sledgehammer). As the Alpha Company commander, I was responsible for all classes of supply (food, water, clothing, fuel, ammunition, construction materials, repair parts, explosives, personal hygiene items, and more). Anything that someone would need except for medical supplies, our company provided it for the 3rd Brigade Combat Team of nearly five thousand soldiers conducting an invasion. When people think of Iraq, they think of the "green zone" with established bases, services, and internet connections. They do not think about the initial invasion where you either took everything you needed or hoped it would be supplied later when rounds were flying. There were no services and no connectivity to home.

I know that being a logistics commander is not as sexy as being an Apache pilot, an Abrams tank commander, a special forces commander, or a ranger company commander. When you think of Army combat and when you think of those susceptible to witness trauma firsthand, that is what probably comes to mind. You do not think of a logistics commander. But I would like to put a few examples into perspective. Imagine that I am your commander, and I tell you that you are going to drive a five-thousand-gallon fuel tanker across the battlefield during a tank battle, and you have to get close to the fight so you can refuel them to keep going. It is not hard to imagine that being hit by the enemy in a fuel tanker could easily turn into a huge fireball. Imagine me having you drive the truck of all the ammunition and explosives, and that can easily be a "fireworks show" nobody wants to be a part of.

Fortunately for our unit and with careful planning and movement precision, I did not lose a single vehicle to the examples mentioned above. However, the threat and the paranoia were there. Instead, what we witnessed firsthand was the destruction of the greatest fighting force ever known to man, significantly destroying the enemy along its path. It was having our unit shot at on every movement. Yet this was not as traumatic as seeing many dead bodies in real life. Seeing body part scattered, blood everywhere, burned bodies, and seeing people (even if they were the enemy) suffering in the process of dying and hearing the screams. That was traumatic! For me, all this was traumatic to include the first time I was shot at, feeling pinned down, feeling there was no way out. I can count four distinct times during the invasion that I almost lost my life and with thoughts going through my mind that this was it for me. The engagements with the enemy, the sending of soldiers on missions, and having them become Missing in Action (MIA) for a short period of time to passing out from exhaustion on the battlefield and waking up in what I can only describe as horrific panic are pretty much how I can describe the series of traumatic events of this invasion.

Then it became worse when I was given more elements to command where my unit grew from 140 to 210 soldiers. One of the elements was a mortuary affairs unit. This is where all Killed-in-Action (KIA) soldiers would come to be processed to be sent home or at least medevaced out from our location. We had to identify them, submit the initial report, and account for personal effects. I will never forget the first person we received; it was a Sergeant First Class (SFC/E-7) who had half of his face blown off and missing his right arm. I assisted in accounting for his personal effects. I pulled his wallet out of his back pocket and had to inventory everything inside. I do not know what was more traumatic, seeing this soldier blown up as badly as he was or seeing the picture of his wife and four children in his wallet. It messed with me for a while.

The 3rd BCT led the battles of Nasiriyah, Samawah, and Karbala and swept around the west side of Baghdad to come into the north since the 4th Infantry Division were not allowed to come in through Turkey. Once we secured Baghdad, we ran resupply missions (often under fire) and attempted to establish the first strongholds and bases in the area for American troops. However, it was not long before the Iraq government was overthrown, and we had to establish an interim government in its place. We would not be that force to help set up the interim government and establish new Rules of Engagement (ROE). Instead, by July 2003, we were relieved by another unit, and we redeployed to Kuwait to turn equipment in, write awards, turn in weapons, and "decompress" for thirty days before going home. We basically ate and wrote reports. But we had almost daily psychological evaluations. I guess we were earmarked as a "high risk" unit that needed to decompress before going home. It did not work though. Once soldiers started speculating that the psychiatrists were standing in their way from boarding an aircraft and going home, suddenly, none of us had a problem in the world.

Processing Trauma

"Then they cried to the Lord in their trouble, and he delivered them from their distress. He brought them out of darkness and the shadow of death and burst their bonds apart. Let them thank the Lord for his steadfast love, for his wondrous works to the children of man" (Psalm 107:13–15 NIV).

The idea that we can process trauma is difficult for me. I think part of what makes something traumatic is that we simply find it impossible to process. Or at least that is what I thought for a long time. The first time I experienced a traumatic incident, I was in a state of shock. It was almost like an out-of-body experience where everything seemed to happen in slow motion. I can tell people were trying to talk to me, but I could not comprehend what they were saying. The graphic images consumed my every waking moment and even in my dreams. I could not think, focus, or do anything because that situation monopolized every brain cell. I became imprisoned to it, lost to it, and I had no idea what was happening to me. It is terrifying thinking back to it. I will not share with you my most traumatic event in combat, but it haunted me 24–7.

In combat, you do not have time to process a traumatic event. You somehow must find a way to move forward, called by the sense of mission, realizing it was a matter of life and death. What happens often is those who serve in combat and experience trauma find a way to suppress it by being distracted by the mission. But that is not healthy; it's just necessary. What happens to most people in combat is that the next traumatic event is right around the corner. It could happen the same day, the next day, often unexpected. Many soldiers I have served with suffer from multiple traumatic events: a series of horrific experiences suppressed within them. Eventually, they will come to surface and will take over their mind.

The more I was exposed to similar situations, I would no longer become shocked as I would become desensitized. The more I became desensitized, the more it became my new normal. The more it became a new normal, the less life meant to me. When life no longer has value, you have reached a point of complete darkness in life.

Taking someone's life, even though justified in war, is extremely traumatic. It simply is not a normal thing to do. As much as we would like to glorify it and are entertained by it on television, taking someone's life is not a very glorious act. It is horror to be shot at and to kill others. The military is now calling wounds like this moral injury. Moral injury is an action that transgresses your deeply held moral beliefs and your expectations. The traumatic impact is the closer you are to the target, the deeper the impact is. In other words, someone who stabs someone to death on the battlefield is different than someone who drops a bomb. Both are moral injuries and can be traumatic, but seeing loss of life, especially firsthand from taking that life, is scarring.

Postdeployment

War is not new; it has been around since the beginning of man when Adam and Eve's children were part of the first recorded murder of humanity. You have heard of the story; it was when Cain killed his brother Abel (Genesis 4:1–16). Man has been killing one another ever since. We have even glorified it in movies. Each time, however, the different types of wounds, which often are compounding, come about. Most of these wounds throughout history went unaddressed. Many who served did not come home, which impacted families and those they served with. Many service members did not come back the same, and many never really fit back into society. It is a historical problem. I personally believe that a person who survives war experiences and must win two wars: the war itself and the war back home. Some win the first and lose the second. I am not sure I fully realized this pertained to me too, but it did. After all, I was a commander. I was the one who needed to help my soldiers. I thought I was above that. But I was humbled in the realization that I was wounded too and losing the battle.

I remember my flight home with anticipation. I wanted to get home to my wife and daughter. I fell asleep on the plane and woke up in the same panic that I became accustomed to, this time frantically looking for my weapon, not knowing where I was. In a weird way, a couple of chuckles from soldiers around me helped me regain my bearing, and my panic shifted to a little embarrassment. What I did not see coming was this was just the beginning of a dark path I would go down.

My trauma from war was compounded by a family crisis upon my return. I came down the steps and, like every soldier, tried to find my family in the crowd as we needed to get in formation to march before a welcome home ceremony. I was no different as a commander. I found my eyes scanning the crowd until we receive the announcement in formation that we were released. That was when everything became a blur, and I saw spouses jumping into the arms and embracing their loved ones. But my wife was not there. Again, I found myself in shock. My father approached me and said she was in

Mexico and knew about my return home and chose not to be here. Long story short, she already made up her mind to leave me and did not want to show up and give me a false expectation. Obviously, we were headed for divorce. I returned to a home with no wife, my daughter with her grandmother, an empty bank account (actually -$565), and dealing with Post-Traumatic Stress.

Here came the second war that very few people like to talk about. I received several mandatory briefings from people about reintegrating back into the family. They said things will be different; your family is used to a routine without you. I came home to none of that. The realization is that 90 percent of all marriages failed after that invasion. That is the statistic I was able to find in an article I read anyways. Reality check! I cannot name a single marriage that survived it. Not one in my unit. Yet I saw many videos of families tying yellow ribbons around trees and great welcome home videos of celebrations of families being reunited. It is what every soldier looked forward to. Even though I didn't get that, I was happy for others who did. We often do not look past that video though. I think it is because it shows a vastly different story.

For those who have returned from war and your family is still intact, I say congratulations. You must admit it is rare, and I am confident to state that you most assuredly had your rough patches. For anyone who experienced trauma, your family will not understand you. They will start off intending to be supportive, but that will be short-lived. It is because they all have a different expectation of what your return would be like. You will not measure up to that expectation. Not only that, you will struggle with readjusting back home. Struggling with readjustment, false expectations, Post-Traumatic Stress, or any of the compounding effects of any of the types of wounds previously mentioned is a bad combination.

There are many books that focus on reintegration; that will not be my focus here. I recommend supplementing this material with a reintegration book that will be helpful for your ministry. The reason why I will not focus on reintegration is simple. I was not good at it returning from any of my deployments because I was wounded every time. When I see others struggle with readjusting, it is because they are wounded too. Therefore, my focus in ministry is on engaging them and helping them through their H3 cycle. The more a warrior can address their wounds and their hurting, the more they can start healing, and then they can start helping others. This will give them purpose (a mission) back home and help them reintegrate.

Traumatic Event Model

"A Psalm of David. The Lord is my shepherd; I shall not want. He makes me lie down in green pastures. He leads me beside still waters. He restores my soul. He leads me in paths of righteousness for his name's sake. Even though I walk through the valley of the shadow of death, I will fear no evil, for you are with me; your rod and your staff, they comfort me. You prepare a table before me in the presence of my enemies; you anoint my head with oil; my cup overflows" (Psalm 23:1–6 NIV).

Trauma is a root word in Greek meaning "wound." In chapter 2, we discussed the types of wounds. Trauma is a psychological/emotional wound. You can also have physical trauma, which goes back to the Greek root word. In the model I presented previously, we classify physical wounds separately from psychological/emotional because of the specialization on how they are treated. Think about a doctor having to treat physical wounds and a psychologist having to treat psychological/emotional wounds. For a veteran or first responders, sometimes, we feel we can treat our wounds ourselves and will only seek help when we think our wound is too serious for us to know what to do. Here is another model that explains more what it is like for a warrior to experience trauma and his/her attempt to deal with it. How can you process what you have seen or done and not end up in complete darkness? How do I come out of it? The traumatic event "hurting" model below illustrates the cycle I have seen so many soldiers go through:

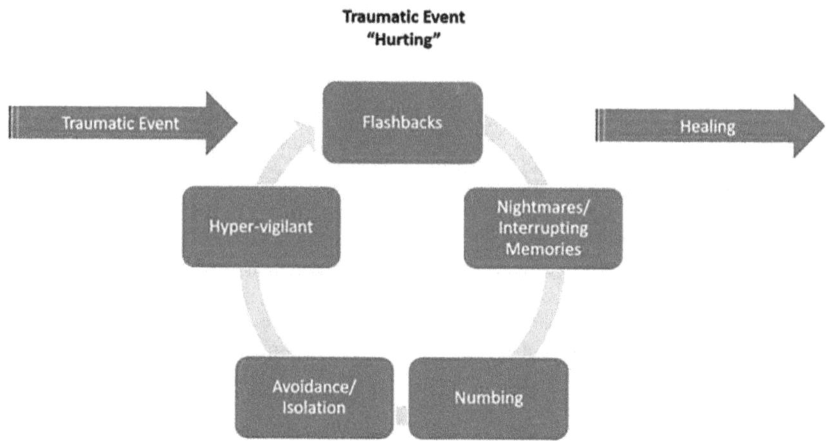

This cycle is typical when a warrior experiences a traumatic event. Let's use an example of Steve, who was a soldier having his battle buddy Mark, his best friend, get shot right next to him and die in his arms. If you have not experienced this, then I want you to imagine your best friend. You are deploying together and promise to have each other's back. Now he is dead. Can we agree that this is a traumatic event? What happens to Steve is a common "cycle of hurting" from this psychological/emotional wound. The traumatic event results in a circular series of flashbacks, nightmares, interrupting memories during the day, an overall numbing effect that leads to avoidance and isolation and becoming hypervigilant. As crazy as this is going to sound, Steve's world is spinning out of control, but it is something that he is trying to deal with himself. He will continue to spin through this on his own because he thinks he can handle it. But really, he is going to fail.

First, just about every warrior has a "type A" personality. We are ingrained in a culture that teaches us to "suck it up and drive on" and to never fail, never quit, and achieve victory at all costs. We pick one another up and, in a "brotherly way," kick one another in the butt when needed to move on. We never show weakness, and we are always competitive. Military culture is not conducive to addressing "invisible" wounds. The military has changed over the past two decades because they are realizing that our psychological/

emotional wounds are a serious issue. So we are starting to talk about it more. However, the Department of Defense and the Veterans Administration still struggle with how to deal with trauma. Failure to address these wounds in a reasonable amount of time without having compounding behavior issues that affect mission readiness is a challenge. Most will be separated from the military, which will only further compound their issues.

Multiple Traumatic Events Model

"The Lord is near to the brokenhearted and saves the crushed in spirit. Many are the afflictions of the righteous, but the Lord delivers him out of them all." (Psalm 34:18–19 NIV)

Therefore, Steve needs help immediately, and he does not really want it. Before I go through solutions, I want you to know that most people I talk to and have served with do not experience a single traumatic event. I have spoken with law enforcement officers who may have a single traumatic event, such as a loss of a partner, someone they could not save in a traffic accident, etc. Most of these are sporadic throughout someone's career. In these cases, the above model applies. But I want to focus on Steve because he is still in harm's way. In the process of carrying Mark's body to an extraction point, he sees a series of traumatic events of people in his unit being wounded and killed. He then placed Mark's body at a casualty collection point and carried on with his mission. Steve goes on and experiences many traumatic events, battle after battle, during his deployment. None of these wounds are being addressed until he gets the opportunity to redeploy back home.

Look at the previous model again. Steve is going through this "circle of hurting" now with many traumatic events consuming him in a time that he is trying to be happy about his return home to his family. Everything is a blur to him. The following model shows what he is experiencing with multiple (compounding) traumatic events.

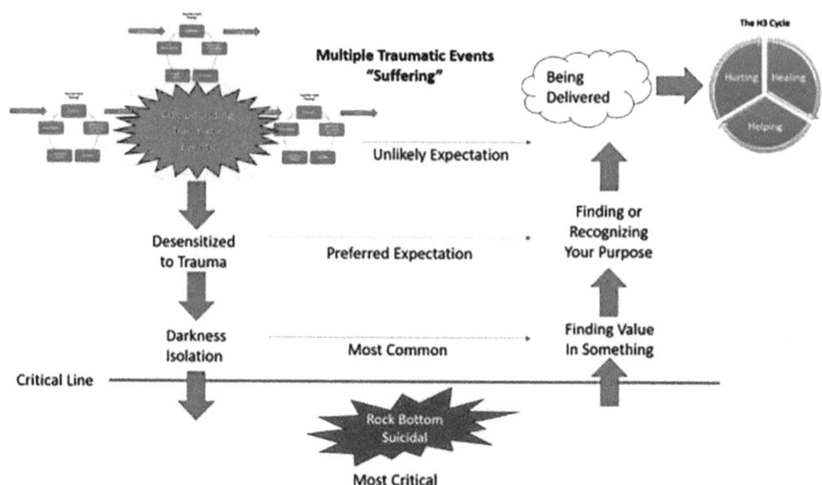

I know this is a complex model, so let us go through it briefly. We mentioned before that Steve was going through his "circles of hurting" from multiple traumatic events. He is now home after his deployment and still juggling expectations of family, friends, and coworkers. It is an unlikely expectation that Steve is just going to handle this on his own, but he tried. He tried when he was still "downrange" on his deployment before becoming somewhat desensitized to the multiple traumatic events he was facing. Do not confuse desensitization with him being able to handle all the trauma he has faced. Although it might appear so, he really has entered a new norm of his expectations. He now recognizes multiple traumatic events as becoming a normal state of his life. He is really becoming good at suppressing the trauma. Upon his return home, the most preferred expectation (outcome) is that he seeks professional help and can recognize his purpose back home and in his life. Spiritually he can be delivered from it and can now navigate through the H3 cycle.

The more common reality for Steve is that he will enter a stage of "darkness" and isolation. This is what happens to most warriors who experience multiple traumatic events. We still believe we can handle what we experienced ourselves, and we do not realize the impact we are having on those around us. Problems only compound from here, and Steve goes into isolation, shutting himself off from the world as much as he can trying to deal with his personal issues, his wounds. He obviously needs professional help, but Steve most likely will not seek it. Having someone in his life who can relate to what he is going through can help him find value in something other than the trauma that has consumed him. If he can find value in anything (a child, a hobby, a project, a new goal, etc.), it can lead to him finding his purpose (preferably God's purpose) and become delivered (divinely) from this. Then he can move on living within his H3 cycle.

I put isolation and darkness together for a reason. Every person (to include myself) describes their time of isolation relatively the same. They will describe it as being "in a place of darkness" or "being in a dark place" or something along those words. This essentially means that they now have a compound wound. You already know that Steve has several psychological/emotional wounds (multiple traumatic events). Now it has become a social wound because he cannot deal with his trauma with the people around him. To make matters worse, Steve's isolation from people now creates a spiritual wound. This is one of the most overlooked wounds I have seen in the psychological field. Far too often, this is treated with drugs (antidepressants). I am not disagreeing with psychologists' treatments here; they are needed, and they are the professionals. But I relate it to being given morphine when you had your leg blown off. You may not feel the pain as much, but the wound is still there, and you still need to stop the bleeding.

A warrior who is in darkness is losing the spiritual battle because he is wounded and bleeding spiritually. Satan is taking over his life. That is why it is often described as being in a "dark place" because he *is* in a spiritually dark place. Guilt, remorse, depression, hopelessness, helplessness, and sadness all compounded by his other types of wounds in isolation is Satan having this warrior, regardless of his spiritual background, in his claws. The claws of Satan are now ripping him to shreds.

For many, far too many, their isolation falls below what I call the critical line. It can be argued that Steve was in critical condition from the beginning of experiencing trauma, but he thought he could handle it. Now he has lost all hope. Some may have sought help and felt it didn't help, but many are still in isolation, and getting help is not even a thought. When someone like Steve drops below the critical line, he will need either direct intervention, or he will die. Veteran suicide happens here. A veteran has experienced death around him. Many have taken life, so taking their own is not a far reach to get to and is often a perceived solution when all else seems to have failed. If someone can intervene for Steve to get him help, then perhaps he can find value in something, find his purpose, and be delivered from darkness to then live within the H3 cycle. If not, he will not make it.

On a brighter note, most warriors do not fall below the critical line. They often recover from isolation. Unfortunately, it does not come without a lot of loss. Some lose their careers, their marriage, their family, lose time, money, and the life they once knew. Their recovery project usually involves rebuilding their life into what it will become. Ideally, they use those experiences for godly purpose. That takes ministry intervention, not only somewhere along the phase of hurting but through the phase of healing and into the phase of serving again.

Postdeployment Ministry

"For the weapons of our warfare are not of the flesh but have divine power to destroy strongholds" (2 Corinthians 10:4 NIV).

Whether you are reading this as a chaplain or a pastor, postdeployment ministry is the largest-growing ministry area. Yet we have not even scratched the surface of meeting warrior needs. We are losing a veteran every sixty-five minutes to suicide. Practically every military family has been destroyed when a veteran experienced trauma while deployed. Many have compounding wounds that are further complicated with substance abuse, destroyed families, and military separation. While on active duty, they had military chaplains that were arguably underused. Postdeployment, chaplains are still largely underused.

Underutilization of military chaplains is due to a variety of reasons. First, remember that veterans think they can handle issues on their own. The higher someone's rank is, the less likely they will go and see a chaplain, especially if that chaplain is of a subordinate rank. Second, most veterans do not attend church services on base. They attend in the town they live in with their families. Third, they mostly do not interact with military chaplains unless they are deployed or if they are attending a mandatory briefing postdeployment. There are other services that, quite frankly, are not even at the forefront of most veterans' minds. Even the most devout Christians seek a local church off base and are connected more with their local pastor than they are with a military chaplain. Finally, chaplains are often overworked and undermanned to completely connect with their population.

Churches have another complex issue with addressing veterans' needs. Pastors are not trained to deal with trauma. They are theologians, and their seminary education does not prepare them to counsel a veteran suffering from the effects of war. As well-meaning as most try to be, they often find themselves out of their element. Instead, they refer veterans to get help from a psychologist. The issue is that psychologists typically do not address the spiritual component. When I refer someone to a psychologist, I refer them to a Christian psychologist. Even then, I am not sure if they are really having their spiritual needs met. Churches typically honor their veterans, are proud to have them in their church families, and often minister to their families. But when a soldier is suffering from trauma, they do not get the support they need from church. Suffering veterans will lose interest in church, stop going, or if they do go, they are quiet. Veterans will quietly come in and quietly leave. I would even argue that they may listen to your message conceptionally, but the message will be discarded. Very few churches have military ministries, fewer have veterans' services, and most just honor veterans on Veterans Day and Memorial Day. Other churches would just like a veteran to start a small group in hope that this will meet all their veteran needs; it will not. Most churches also give a standard evangelical salvation message weekly, which further disconnects a veteran who has heard it many times before. In reality, they are dealing with shaken faith, and they will inevitably lose interest.

That is why I believe there is a need for a different form of ministry for veterans. I formed Serve Ministries Inc. to build community chaplains to meet veterans' needs. They help establish and lead support groups, military Bible studies, and meet with veterans one-on-one. Community chaplains are aggressively assertive, realizing that the veterans they are trying to help will go quiet and isolate themselves. They are specifically trained in trauma. It is a "ministry of presence" and constant contact with the veteran. I often say a chaplain can probably handle about a handful of veterans if they are war-torn. I recruit other veterans mature in the faith to become chaplains. A majority were never chaplains in the military. I like that most of them were not. I prefer warriors who experienced the same wounds as someone they are going to minister to. There is a reason for this; I strongly believe it takes a veteran to heal a veteran. One of my greatest advantages when talking to a veteran who served in Iraq is that I have been to Iraq too. The same when it goes for being an Afghanistan veteran. When you can mutually share where you were in those countries, it brings more credibility to them than a certification or degree on your wall. I am not saying that those are not important because they are as well. But this is about relatability.

Confession time. When I went to psychologists coming back from my deployments to Iraq and Afghanistan, the first thing I tried to do was discredit them. I am not saying that was right; I am saying that is what I did. It was simple in my mind: if you have not been through what I have been through, then how do you think you are going to help me? You just do not understand. You might be sympathetic or empathize with me, but I do not want that. I want someone I can relate to and can understand me when I am talking. I cannot say that this position is healthy. I am sure each of those psychologists meant well and could have helped to a point. I was simply not going to let them because I could not relate to them any more than they could relate to me. The same goes with pastors, ministers, or any other professional service trying to help me. I cannot tell you how many veterans feel the same, but most do.

Review Questions

1. Y/N You can completely recover from a traumatic event? Why or why not?
2. Trauma is what type of wound?
3. Explain the "cycle of hurting" and how someone can overcome it to start healing.
4. What does it mean to "be delivered" from multiple traumatic events, and do you think it is necessary? Why or why not?
5. Do you believe a chaplain or a minister needs to assert themselves into the life of someone suffering from trauma? Explain.
6. Explain how a veteran who has experienced multiple traumatic events can help others in the H3 cycle.
7. Do you believe churches today are prepared and effective at meeting veterans' needs? Please explain.

CHAPTER 4

SLIPPING INTO ISOLATION

Two people are better off than one, for they can help each other succeed. If one person falls, the other can reach out and help. But someone who falls alone is in real trouble.

—Ecclesiastes 4:9–10

Isolation

As discussed in the previous chapter, "isolation" is quite common for a veteran or first responder who has experienced traumatic events. You need to be able to recognize the signs of slipping into isolation so you can prevent that from happening to you. Otherwise, you will not be effective in your purpose that God has given you. Likewise, you need to recognize it in others so you can proactively engage them. The *Oxford Dictionary* defines *isolation* as "the process or fact of isolating or being isolated." I do not think that definition really fits well, nor is it complete when referring to what isolation really is. For the purposes of this discussion, I humbly propose defining isolation the following way: isolation is the process of willingly or unwillingly disconnecting with people around you.

This definition represents the heart of what we are really trying to point out. Some people who serve chose to distance themselves.

I see this more commonly with police officers, especially when they live in the community that they serve in. They know they are held to a higher standard, and they consciously choose to isolate themselves from the public. However, others cannot help it. They "slip" through a gradual process of isolating themselves from others because they feel they either "need time to think" or they find that being around people is raising their anxiety level. They cannot control it; they simply go into isolation because it is better than the alternative of being around people.

Police Officers

For law enforcement officers, I think the issue really surrounds working long hours, having a traumatic event, and processing it with homelife and additional shifts on the job. Police officers never truly leave from their operational environment. Every police officer tries to balance family life with their next shift on patrol. Isolation creeps in like a thief in the night. Next thing you know, you are just working and going home. You no longer want to participate in family events, activities, or even conversations. On the job, it is all business, and you no longer have a desire to talk to your fellow officers. Depression sets in, and you go into isolation.

Officer Stephens went on a police call of a suspected homicide. He was the first on the scene. When he went into the house, he saw the victim, an eleven-year-old girl. She had been brutally killed. It was a mess that seriously impacted him. As other first responders arrived, he did his best to collect the information he needed so he could write his police report. He went home that evening and did not tell his family. His twelve-year old daughter goes to school the next day and finds out one of her friends was killed. She was mortified and came home from school that day crying. Officer Stephens came home later that evening when his shift was over to find his daughter crying to her mother.

The situation was already traumatic. Every time he remembered the events, it reminded him of his daughter. He even had a nightmare the night before that it happened to his daughter. He panics when he walks into the bedroom and sees his daughter crying, wondering what happened. To learn that the victim was his daughter's friend further affects him. Fortunately, his daughter is talking about it with her mother. She is going to have counselors coming into her school. She is terribly upset, but she has support and, over time, should not be severely traumatized from this experience.

The same cannot be said for Officer Stephens. He does not tell his family that he was first on the scene. His reason was that he did not think it would help. So he keeps it to himself. A homicide detective is assigned to the case to find a suspect, but he has no leads. The detective questions the parents who left the child alone to run an errand. While they were away, it appears someone broke into the house and killed their daughter. It was a senseless crime that really made no sense.

Officer Stephens takes personal interest in the case, but it is not his lane. It was the case for the homicide detective now. Within the same week, he responds to a baby drowning, a fatal traffic accident, and a teenager who overdosed on drugs. He starts to distance himself from his family and others. He is having a difficult time making sense of it all. He refuses to go to church with his family that weekend, appears agitated and short-tempered, and wants to be left alone.

What do you think Officer Stephens is dealing with?

This is an example that is quite common among police officers. Police officers are faced with bad news daily. They are called first responders for a reason: they run toward the bad news. A case like this is common. As the chaplain of the Niceville Police Department, I can tell you that police officers deal with worse situations that happen in our community daily. I have been on countless ride-alongs with our police officers because this gives me the best opportunity to minister to them one-on-one. I have responded to fires, traffic accidents, and even a baby drowning. I have had to minister to the police officers as well as the victim's family members.

Investigator John Lee allowed me to use this story:

Baby Drownings

Within a two-day span, my team was alerted to two separate baby death calls. One was a drowning in a pool, and the other was a drowning in scalding tub water. The pool death was an unfortunate, heartbreaking accident. The second will haunt me forever.

When I arrived on scene, it was utter chaos. Several small children ran around the front of the house unsupervised. The adults of the vacation rental were separated, awaiting their turn at an interview with me. I immediately called the Child Advocacy Center and requested help to take care of the small children on scene. It seemed like merely seconds when a carload of child protection team members arrived and saved me. They jumped out of the car, saw where I pointed, and started wrangling the children. As fast as the team arrived, they whisked away the children for medical and mental evaluations. I said a short prayer and steered myself to the front door. All had been evacuated from the home except the poor child. When I entered the front door, the blood ran from my face. My chief was sitting in a chair and leaned over the child on the floor, with his face in his hands. I thought I had lost my chief. I did not think he would come back from this. But he did. He rallied like the leader we needed most at that time and started taking care of his team while we worked this horrid scene.

I forced myself to study the baby. I had to find something, anything that would allow me to champion this poor child. The child lay motionless on the floor with most of his poor head and body scalded to the point the first layer of skin had come off.

I spent several weeks working this case. In the end, I could not convince the state to move forward, making someone stand up in front of a judge and explain why they neglected this child to the point of letting him drown in scalding hot water.

I failed this child. God tells me there were reasons, but they are beyond my comprehension.

I had to respond to this scene as the chaplain. I had to minister to the police officers on the scene and to the family. It was not a good day for the department. There was mixed emotion from great sadness to immense anger. Police officers wanted justice, and the family was in shock. I did the best I could to talk to the family that was visiting from out of town. I also knew ministering to the police officers involved would be ongoing for some time.

Police officers really do not get to escape their environment; they live in it. They can respond to a traffic accident on their street corner and respond to a homicide on the same block they live on. They pass those locations on the way home when they get off shift and pass by them again when they start their next shift. It only makes them more sensitive to what is happening around them. On an unrelated note, I think that is why many police officers prefer to live in a different town that they patrol in.

One of the keys things I look for is the way the police officer reacts. I am looking for several things:

- Is the police officer showing emotion over the case—anger, frustration, crying—or completely unbothered by the situation? Personally, the latter is most concerning to me. A normal person will react.
- How is the police officer acting in the days to come? Is he/she appearing to go about their duties normally, or do we see a change in their behavior/discipline? If there is a change to what is normal for them, then that can be an indicator. I look for signs such as the officer is usually a jokester but now is not joking. Maybe the officer is a talkative person and now seems uninterested in talking. I am looking for any sign to what is not normal for them. If I sense that they are not acting normal, it is time for me to engage with them.
- Next I will bring up the situation several days later to see their reaction. A normal response would be, "That was a sad case" or "I cannot even imagine what that family is going through." However, an evasive response like "I do not want to talk about it, chaplain!" or "Every time someone brings it up, it just pisses me off" may be an indication that I need to engage with them.

There are signs that someone is isolating themselves. You will see a change in behavior. I do not care how smooth someone thinks they are and how well they try to hide it. They will not be able to cover it up if they are in isolation. They have experienced a traumatic event, which is probably resulting in some compounding wounds from psychological/emotional and there either is, or they are well on the way to having a social wound. It is also quite easy to tell because people universally act somewhat the same when they go into isolation: they do not act normal.

As chaplains, we need to get to know our officers. You do not need to know everything about them or even be friends, but you had to have been around them enough to know what is normal. However, I have had relationships with leadership where they will come to me and let me know when someone is not acting normal. It also helps to promote a culture where the officers look out for one another. I had an officer that was concerned about a fellow officer and brought his concern to me instead of his chain of command. He did not want him to get into trouble, but he wanted him to talk to someone. All three of these circumstances place me in a position where I can engage and evaluate how the police officer reacts.

Important Note. Police officers will not seek help if they are slipping into isolation. Police officers will seek help before it gets to that point if they seek it at all. Isolation occurs when the officer thinks he can handle the situation him/herself. This is usually done by suppressing emotions, thinking it will go away over time. Sometimes it does, but isolation occurs when wounds starts consuming you.

Active Military/Veterans

For people who serve or have served in the military, it works a little different than police officers. I think the main reason is that we deploy somewhere else. The trauma we deal with does not come from our community. We deploy to some distant land, fight our wars, and then redeploy back home. I think this makes veterans more susceptible to family isolation. Let me give you a few examples and reasons why this is the case. When the initial invasion of Iraq occurred in 2003, the average deployment time was about six months. From 2007 to 2009, the average deployment went up to fifteen months with some units being deployed as many as eighteen months. I heard stories about guys deploying when their wife was pregnant and came home to a toddler that was already walking and talking.

I remember my first deployment as a new company commander. It was in 2002 to patrol the Iraqi/Kuwaiti border while the UN weapons inspectors were trying to inspect Iraqi nuclear facilities. We deployed for six months, then redeployed home for eighty-two days before having to deploy again to Kuwait to launch the invasion of Iraq that would kick off Operation Iraqi Freedom. That lasted another six months. I remember when I saw my daughter when I returned, and I looked into her eyes, and she got scared because she did not recognize me. It upset her, and it upset me.

As previously stated, war is not normal even though it has existed since the beginning of human history. Killing and destruction just are not normal no matter how much we try to glorify it. It is traumatic! People are used to seeing it on TV, which desensitizes them to the point that they cannot relate. When a veteran returns home from a deployment, he/she literally leaves the battlefield where killing became a norm to the home front where it is truly abnormal. When I returned from my deployment, the single most aggravating thing that bothered me were people. Naturally, I was already affected by my homecoming and how screwed up that was. But people really irritated me for no other reason than they were acting normal. They were going about their normal lives like there was no war going on, and it really aggravated me. It really did not make sense that people did not realize that in Iraq, people were shooting, and people were dying every day.

It made me angry to see people happy and carrying on while I knew what was going on over there. I even felt guilty for being home. I felt guilty for coming home alive when others did not. I even questioned why I came home to such a screwed-up environment when it appeared those who came home in flag-draped coffins had more to live for. I did not like how I felt. My new understanding is that I was suffering from PTSD and inability to readapt being home with so many issues that it led to my isolation. I did not want it, but I was not functioning and handling everything well. I felt better by myself. I felt that people were looking at me funny; maybe they realized I came home different. But I could not get my mind off from being in Iraq and what I experienced there. I even remember wanting to go back more than wanting to be home. Not because of some sense of duty or obligation (even though I said that often) but because things just made more sense to be in Iraq than they did at home. I obviously needed help.

So for me, I welcome the time by myself rather than being around people. I did not realize that it was leading me to darkness. Isolation is a slippery slope toward destruction. Your family will not understand; nobody except those who were with you over there can relate. When you shut yourself off from the world, Satan is lurking around the corner. The problems will only mount. Destroyed relationships with family, old friends, old acquaintances occur next. Divorce is highly likely during this time. Prolonged effects start impacting job performance. For many years, the military would just separate people suffering from PTSD. They are better at getting veterans help today, but we have a long way to go with few real solutions.

This may come as a shock, but isolation is a very normal response for someone dealing with PTSD and the inability to process normalcy at home. The veteran simply cannot relate to their environment, so they go isolated. Too many "professionals" wanted to lock a guy like me up in a padded cell or drug me as if I was suffering from some sort of paranoid schizophrenia or something. People around me thought I was "crazy," and now I know better. I was neither, and I did not need a padded cell or drugs. I needed help for the trauma I experienced, but I also needed help to adjust back to everyday life. I was just trying to handle it through quiet time, away from people, to try to understand it. What I did not realize, as most veterans do not realize, is that this approach does not work.

A Solution

"I consider that our present sufferings are not worth comparing with the glory that will be revealed in us" (Romans 8:18 NIV).

I have eluded to the solution for some time. A solution is supported by the opening verse. I am careful not to call this "the solution," for I am not so bold to make such a proclamation. I am only proposing a solution. The one slipping into isolation thinks they can handle their situation themselves. They do not realize they are losing that battle. That is where the battle buddy needs to come in—the chaplain, the mentor, the pastor, the minister, the friend, they need to come in. Just as Ecclesiastes 4:9–10 starts off with "Two people are better off than one…" it also means the one is not isolated. Due to the realization that the one wants to be left alone, that is where I promote "assertive ministry" and call on those whom I mentor to aggressively engage the one you are trying to serve because they will not come to you. Far too often, I see people in ministry expecting people to come to them for help. Ask yourself, How often do people reach out to you when they need help? Be honest! How many people close to you have struggled with an issue only for you to later find out about it? Your reaction was probably like most, "Why didn't you call me?" You were willing to be there for them, but they did not call you.

For chaplains, I say it is our job to know. We need to seek them out and "assert" ourselves into their situation. The biggest issue I have with mentoring chaplains on this is that they do not think they have it in them to assert themselves in other people's life. Too many chaplains want to take a passive approach and listen when other people want to talk to them. That certainly is a technique, and there are certainly times for that. But you will never reach anyone that way who really needs help. When someone wants to isolate themselves, you "being there" takes that away from them. You "coming back around" prevents it. You cannot "be there" for someone if you are not there. They cannot go into isolation if you are there. Naturally, you will not be able to be with them 24-7. But you can be there regularly, and you can also encourage others around him to remain engaged.

Preventing Matters from Getting Worse

Extraordinarily little positive comes from isolation. One would argue that a little "me time" is needed. That is not isolation. Isolation is a clear avoidance or ignoring other people. It is more continuous and is abnormal to how they usually act and interact with others. When someone slips into isolation, they are on the path to damaging relationships, and the result are social wounds.

My social wounds when I came back from Iraq were a result of coming home to a situation different than I left it. It was not how I envisioned my return, and everything had changed. There was little support to prevent me from going into isolation, and I was not going to create more social wounds than I immediately received from my return. I was leaving my unit for a Permanent Change of Station (PCS) move to a new assignment, and my family was already disbursed.

For most, they returned to what they thought would be normal. They had a nice welcome home celebration filled with happiness, anticipation, cheers, and a hope for reconnection. The "honeymoon" period wears off, and soon the realization sets in that your family has been handling day-to-day routines without you. Many times, they established new ways of doing things while you were gone. They adapted to a life without you. Now you are back, and in sorts, you have interrupted their routine. They may be doing things a different way than you would have. That may have changed your rules or your ways, and they like the way they have things established now better than the way you did. Circumstances may have changed with new hobbies, family activities, new pets, new major purchases, a new child (for those who deployed when they had a pregnant spouse), the spouse may have a new job, a teenager may now have a driver's license, a child may have a new boyfriend/girlfriend, or something simple like they painted a wall a different color.

There will be changes that will make the veteran feel like a stranger or a visitor in their own home. They will struggle with where they fit in the routines of those around them. This will cause friction. It only takes a couple of weeks for this to set in. A failure for a veteran to adapt and adjust often leads to family isolation. It also leads to friction, frustration, anger, disappointment, and a feeling of being "lost" even at home. If the veteran is suffering from trauma, their mind is completely preoccupied, which makes them symptomatically incapable of adjusting to change.

Symptoms of Isolation

Some of the symptoms of veteran/first responder going into isolation include the following:

- Going quiet, not engaging in conversations, or even wanting to talk
- Having a location away from people whom he/she spends a majority of their time
- Staring at nothing: a TV turned off, a garden, a tree in the backyard, long stares in a distance
- Being nonresponsive when called or having a noticeable delayed response
- Being jumpy and easily aggravated, angered, or frustrated
- Substance abuse alone (drinking heavily in private, overuse of pain medication, etc.)
- Finding no satisfaction or approval of things happening around them
- Not wanting to go anywhere/do anything
- Not bathing regularly or taking care of themselves
- Showing no interest in things going on around them
- Not eating regular meals and especially not eating around others

This is not an exhaustive list but an important list you can share with family members of veterans who may be going into isolation. An important technique is to ensure the spouse can call you when their veteran is going isolated. Warning! There is a slippery slope here. I had people calling me to complain about their spouse, but that is not the intent. We are not certified marriage counselors, but we can show up when needed if a veteran is isolating themselves. Our job during these times is to be an encourager and to help them talk about their emotions (most of which are normal) and encourage them to engage in activities they find value in.

One thing I know about those who serve is that they like structure. We are almost all wired that way. Those who serve are creatures of habit. We like the adrenaline rush of the unexpected in those moments of action within our occupation, but we still want the routines to be structured. The best way to help someone out of "slipping into isolation" is obviously to be there for them. But we also must help them find value in something again. Remember the multitraumatic model? The way out of isolation is to find value in something. It is also the way out of darkness. It is also the way to prevent the veteran from falling below the "critical line" into darkness. They need something of value.

This is frustrating for family members; they automatically will feel that they are the ones that the veteran must value. Although this certainly should be the case, often, they only add to the problem. That is why the veteran is distancing themselves from his family. Something is not right. It is not working. The veteran is not adapting back into the family, and he/she cannot figure out why. Family pressure combined with a veteran dealing with several compounding wounds is a formula for disaster.

The solution is having someone engage and assertively spend time with them. By doing so, the veteran/first responder is unable to remain in isolation. Your presence suspends that from occurring, even if only temporary. This is the power of ministry—to talk to them. This is also the value of being relatable. I believe, it takes a veteran to heal a veteran, a police officer to heal a police officer, a fireman to heal a fireman, etc. This is ideal, but if you do not have that background, then you being there is better than nobody being there. Do your best and ask on the Lord to give you the right words to say. Compassion and caring go a long way. I am a police chaplain who spent twenty-seven years in the Army. I do not completely relate to my police officers even though I try. But they have grown to respect that I am there and that I try to get a perspective of what they go through. It is less than ideal, but it is better than having nobody.

Engaging Someone in Isolation

"So do not fear, for I am with you; do not be dismayed, for I am your God. I will strengthen you and help you; I will uphold you with my righteous right hand" (Isaiah 41:10 NIV).

Here is what I recommend talking about (these questions are veteran focused but can be tailored for first responders):

- Ask straightforward question starting with, "How are you doing?" (icebreaker).
- Do you have something to drink (quick distracting activity that also is an icebreaker)?
- Do not ask yes/no questions. Ask questions that require the person to talk like, "Why are you sitting outside here by yourself?" I really do not care about the veteran's response as much as I care about getting them to respond and start talking to me.
- "I know you just returned from a deployment. What was it like when you got off the plane?"
- "How do you feel your children are with you being home?"
- "How is your spouse dealing with you being home?"
- "What have you liked about your return home?"
- "What have you not liked about being back home?"
- Additional questions just come about by showing interest in their responses. By this point, the veteran should be "opening up" to you.

I want you to notice what I have not asked the veteran:

- I did not ask any questions about their deployment. If the veteran wants to talk about it, then that is their choice, and it is a time to listen.

- If I know of their traumatic experiences, I do not bring them up because I do not want to trigger them. This is a common error and usually shuts the veteran down from wanting to talk.
- I do not bring up substance abuse even if I know he is doing it.
- I do not bring up problems even if I know what they are.
- I do not bring up comments his/her spouse may have divulged.
- I try not to have any question that suggests to the veteran that he/she is having a problem or any question that can be perceived as an allegation.

Why? Why do I not ask the questions above? It is quite simple. Veterans in isolation think they can handle their issues themselves. As I mentioned previously in this book, they are type A, and they have not asked for help here. They will not want to talk if you are even remotely negative, accusatory, or condemning in your questions. They will no longer want to talk to you, which is counterproductive even if you are right. I also do not want to trigger any PTSD or traumatic thoughts. I do not want to further wound them. Plus, none of this moves them forward; those questions only further entrench them in the past.

The conversation must have a purpose. The purpose is to get them to focus on the here and now. They already are spending all day thinking about what happened to them on their deployment. My goal is to get their mind off that topic. My questions are about their return home up until today. Why? Because this is their current situation, and I want the veteran to be more aware of their environment now. My purpose is to break the cycle of isolationism and return them to meaningful day-to-day tasks and to show value in something. So some follow-on questions are as follows: What did you like to do for fun before you deployed? What are your hobbies? One of my favorite questions, If money were not an issue, what would you do? My purpose is for the veteran to put their sights on something they value. I have had veterans talk about fishing, hunting, sailing, traveling, rebuilding/refurbishing a car, getting a motorcycle to go riding, and all kinds of things. This is perfect discussion to have with a veteran because now they are thinking about something of value.

Getting a veteran to talk about something of value does two particularly important things. First, if you recall the previous chapter, finding something of value prevents them from falling below the critical line into darkness, and it puts them on the path toward the H3 cycle. Second, you have temporarily taken their mind off their issue and given them a positive thought that you can encourage them to pursue right away. Perhaps you may even join them. It is very "therapeutic" that if the veteran wants to go sailing that he/she goes. When it comes to me, I only would ask to go with them if they are a male veteran, which brings me to the golden ministry rule.

Golden ministry rule. I do not go anywhere alone with a female veteran for any reason. If it is a male veteran, then I will spend a lot of one-on-one time with him. If it is a female veteran, I always want to introduce them to a female on my staff whom I can mentor and have her spend the one-on-one time with the female veteran. Under no circumstances should you *ever* violate this rule. You can imagine all the compromising situations this can cause for you personally and to the veteran. Do not go there!

Helpful Pointers

Jesus' words, "I have told you these things, so that in me you may have peace. In this world you will have trouble. But take heart! I have overcome the world" (John 16:33 NIV).

I want you to think through a conversation with a veteran and daydream about it in your mind. I want you to think about the questions of what to ask and not to ask. I want you to think through the purpose of what you are trying to do. Remember you are trying to lead them out of isolation and into finding something of value. Having something of value significantly decreases their chances of falling into darkness. However, this is not one conversation. This must be the first of many conversations.

I will always leave that conversation with a date/time I will be coming back. It is important to me to do that within the next seventy-two hours, preferably the next day. The next time we get together, I want to focus on the event they find value in. Our conversation will be on planning it out and setting a date to do it. That serves a couple of purposes. First, it takes an idea and makes it a reality and a goal. Veterans like to have a plan, and they certainly like to have a mission. Second, it gets them to think through tasks that need to be done to accomplish this mission, so now they have something else to think about. Third, it gives me a chance to ask questions. Veterans like to be a "subject matter expert" in something they value. I try to become the student to learn from them. Fourth, I want them to look forward to fun.

The day of the event, I am excited even if it is something that I may not be completely interested in. I am excited that the veteran is interested in it, and I am keeping an open mind. I am alert, though, Does the veteran look like he is enjoying the activity. If so, great! If not, we need to liven up the conversation.

Here are some other things I try to avoid:

- I personally will turn down alcohol, but I do not forbid it for the veteran. However, it is not a focus either. I do not want it to be a barrier between us, but I will not participate in an event if his goal is to get drunk.
- I try to avoid the conversation from going negative about people, i.e., complaining about his wife, his unit, his problems. We are there to have fun, so I try to keep the conversation positive.
- If he wants to talk about his deployment, I will let him, and I will listen. But I will not let that conversation rule the day, nor do I want that to be the last conversation of the day. I want him to get it off his chest, show compassion for his feelings, and then make the conversation positive again to get past it.
- I do not tell the veteran that I am ministering or mentoring them. He most likely did not ask for it. If he did, I do

not dwell on it and make that a point of importance. I am being a compassionate friend, not taking a stance that I am somehow superior to them.

- I do not let them put me in danger. I will always respectfully decline. Sometimes, "Man, I really do not want to do that" helps set boundaries for safety but is not shutting down the event. Especially if you follow up with a part of the event that you really like that is safer.

Thoughts on Prayers

"May the God of hope fill you with all joy and peace as you trust in him, so that you may overflow with hope by the power of the Holy Spirit" (Romans 15:13 NIV).

I will end an event with a prayer. I want you to realize that the first time I talked to them, I did not do this. It is my personal preference not to. I will be praying for the veteran. But I do not want to get on some evangelical campaign day 1. I only want them to think about something of value that interests them. If they know me well, I will let them ask me to pray for them. Then I will pray with them right there. However, by the event we have established a relationship, then I am going to get a prayer in there because I am trying to get Jesus involved in helping them become delivered from the situation. But that is not what this prayer is going to be about. I will pray for that veteran later. Our prayer together to God is about being thankful for a wonderful day. I personally keep the prayer positive and not about his issues. I will also let him know that I will be continuously praying for them and set up another day to get together.

My personal prayer life is where I take all the negativity that I have heard from my veteran to the Lord. This is called intercessory prayer, and biblically, it is immensely powerful. Again, I am trying to get the veteran to remain positive, moving forward, and find value in something. From that point forward, I am helping them get delivered from their traumatic events and into the H3 cycle. Once I can get him there, then we only need to meet every so often as friends. We may become close friends, but a Sentinel (reference chapter 1) remains on watch. If you are a Sentinel, then you are always evaluating where they are on the H3 cycle. Are they hurting, healing, or helping? What is your goal? Answer: getting them to a place where they are in a "new normal" and helping others. This is God's purpose in whatever way that looks like. When they go through additional hurting or healing, your goal is to help them through that to get them back to helping (serving).

Review Questions

1. In your own words, what does it mean to go into isolation?
2. Are there any differences between police officers and veterans who go into isolation?
3. List three things you should not talk about when having a conversation with someone who is slipping into isolation?
4. What is the primary goal when talking to someone in isolation?
5. What is the golden ministry rule?
6. What are the things you should avoid when attending an event with someone you are ministering to as you help them find value in something?
7. What are your thoughts about praying with a veteran suffering from wounds that is causing them to slip into isolation?

CHAPTER 

CAPTIVE IN DARKNESS

Be sober-minded; be watchful. Your adversary the devil prowls around like a roaring lion, seeking someone to devour.

—1 Peter 5:8 ESV

There is real spiritual warfare, and the *spiritual battleground* is your soul. The single greatest decision someone must make in life is whether they will accept Christ or deny Him. Failure to decide means Satan gets you by default. There is a spiritual battle going on for your soul from the time you are born. It is not God fighting for your soul. He already provided the way through Christ. The default for your soul is Satan because the soul starts out fallen. This was a curse on humanity from the fall of man and the creation of a sin nature than goes back to Adam and Eve. That is why Jesus says that you must be born again of the spirit (read John 3:1–8).

I assume if you are reading this book that you are a believer. However, Satan is not finished even if you have accepted Christ. He may have lost your soul, but his next objective is to destroy your natural life in order that you become unsuccessful in serving God. He wants to derail you from your God-given purpose to save other souls.

Satan wants to take horrible experiences you face and pull you into darkness where he can destroy you. He plays on your shame, regret, fear, mistakes, sin, anger, frustration, loneliness, and compounds that with your wounds. Darkness is a critical state where the person has fallen below the critical line and now living in captivity in darkness. This is a dark and Satanic topic, but it is important that we discuss the impacts and how we need to minister to a veteran or a first responder who is a prisoner in darkness and losing hope. This is also a desperate point for intervention. The clock is ticking, and time is running out. This is where many give up on life.

Suicide is a real issue. The veteran suicide rate is about one every sixty-five minutes or, on average, twenty veteran suicides each day.[1] We have lost more veterans to suicide than to combat operations in the past twenty years. In 2019, 228 police officers committed suicide, which was a 24 percent increase over the previous year. We are losing more police officers to suicide than are being killed in the line of duty.[2] However, you can make a difference. The battle is not lost. What does it say when we lose more veterans and more first responders to suicide than in the line of duty? It is because we need to "see" the larger battle.

> For our struggle is not against flesh and blood, but against the rulers, against the authorities, against the powers of this dark world and against the spiritual forces of evil in the heavenly realms. (Ephesians 6:12 NIV)

The larger battle is not flesh and blood but of spiritual forces of evil. Being in darkness is *losing* the spiritual battle to Satan, but you have not *lost* if you are still alive. Satan's goal is for people to take their own life. God's goal is for people to rebound stronger and to live. I

---

1 Executive Order 13861. "Executive Order on a National Roadmap to Empower Veterans and End Suicide." Retrieved from https://www.whitehouse.gov/presidential-actions/executive-order-national-roadmap-empower-veterans-end-suicide/.

2 Shannon, Joel. 2020. "At least 228 police officers died by suicide in 2019, Blue H.E.L.P. Says. That's more than were killed in the line of duty." *USA Today* (January).

want you to know that God wants to deliver people from darkness. He wants to give them hope. He is the solution. His solution is life and purpose. Satan's solution is death. Far too many are choosing death.

One of the most frustrating questions to field is, "Why would God allow this to happen?" That is a separate discussion. Every person has free will to make their own life decisions. As ministers, we must always promote truth. God does not want them to give into darkness. He wants them to live. The primary reason why Jesus came to this world was to rectify and restore humanity's relationship with God. Man destroyed that relationship, and "the wages of sin is death, but the gift of God is eternal live in Jesus Christ our Lord" (Romans 6:23 NIV). God has a separate plan.

> "For I know the plans I have for you," declares the Lord, "plans to prosper you and not to harm you, plans to give you hope and a future." (Jeremiah 29:11 NIV)

Darkness does not have to end in suicide. Even though there are many veterans and first responders who commit suicide, it does not have to be the result. God wants to redeem people from darkness. He always has, and He always will. I know this personally: a veteran or a first responder can come out of darkness stronger than ever. There is "hope and a future," and Jesus is the real solution. When I was in darkness, I did not see it, and I was a Christian. It took divine intervention, and I almost did not make it. I needed help, and I did not seek it. I was fortunate; far too many are not. For me, I had to die to self. Not a physical one, but since I gave up on life already, the only way for me to live was to surrender my life to God. A biblical verse that I really connected with is this:

> I have been crucified with Christ; and it is no longer I who live, but Christ lives in me; and the life which I now live in the flesh I live by faith in the Son of God, who loved me and gave Himself up for me. (Galatians 2:20 NIV)

I even used this verse during my retirement speech from the Army. It completely describes where I am; I am on borrowed time from God. He could have taken my life on any of my deployments. I certainly was in harm's way multiple times when rounds were flying. I could have succumbed to my darkness and taken my own life. I have so much to praise God for. I owe him everything, and I only now live in the flesh for His will. I am not alone. Some of the strongest people I see in the faith can relate to this verse and this story. They were once in darkness and now have been delivered. Although they are still dealing with wounds in their own H3 cycle, they are the more dedicated servants, in my experience, in the world. They each have a new view on life and have completely turned it over to God. They passionately get up each day to serve Him. I run into so many people that God is raising up in these times to reach those in darkness. Unfortunately, I also run into so many who are not responding to God's call.

Since you are reading this, we need to focus on equipping you with "backup" to help others in darkness. You cannot help someone alone, so do not even try. If they end up taking their life, it will be a crisis that now you have to live with. This thought scares people from committing to their calling. I had a chaplain in our program who quit when I told him this could happen. You must be braver than that and use resources around you. This requires a lot of prayer. Pray for wisdom and strength to serve. This also requires research of local-, city-, state-, and national-level services. For my ministry area, I compile a directory of all the services around me so I can match people with their needs. You will need to do this for your area. A good place to start is understanding what national-level services are offered. They are larger and more resourced. We will cover local resources in the last chapter of this book.

Let us look at national-level organizations and how suicide is handled and what is being done to prevent suicide. All have found varying degrees of success and failure. It is rather simple to be an optimist and say a lot is being done to help veterans. It is also simple to be a pessimist and say it is not working, which is why we have so many suicides occurring. I strive not to be in either camp. I think it is important to realize that we still have a significant issue on our hands. But the solution is to work together and educate people that spiritual warfare is real. Or at least let them respect your position enough to allow you in ministry to have access to the veterans. You will get a lot further in ministry with cooperation. Plus, most of the national-level organizations are far more resourced than you will probably ever be. So it is best to use them.

Department of Defense (DoD) Response to Intervention

I do not personally agree with the military response to intervention of those who contemplate/attempt to commit suicide. It is primary because they only view suicide as a psychological condition in my opinion. By this point, you know that the wounds a veteran is facing are far more than just psychological. I am also disappointed there is not more chaplaincy involvement/engagement. When I mentor chaplains, I am constantly "preaching" to them about engaging veterans. Most will get a little defensive and say they are. In the area of suicide, they really are not. But this is what the military does that I find to be frustrating. When the military identifies any problem, they add classes. Suicide was identified as a problem, and their solution was to offer classes on suicide prevention/resiliency. I like that they often use a military chaplain to give these classes. But when the veteran attempts suicide or states they want to harm themselves, the military response is to "conduct a military operation" to detain the person and lock them up in a mental ward.

I also feel the worst thing you can do to a veteran is confine them against their will. But I get the rationale for placing someone in a mental ward. You want someone to constantly monitor them 24-7 so the veteran does not harm themselves. But you have now compounded the problem if they suffer from trauma. Plus, the treatment that follows detainment is predominantly psychological in nature, consisting primarily with prescribing drugs and providing psychological counseling. Where did the chaplain go? Why isn't he there? I do not have the answers to these questions other than the military does not see suicide for what it really is—being in darkness and losing in spiritual warfare. They see it as a psychological issue. They are simply fighting the wrong battle in my opinion. You now know that the veteran is suffering from multiple wounds, which include psychological/emotional and spiritual. But the veteran may also have physical and social wounds that have taken them into darkness.

Intervention is needed, and in many cases, the veteran does need to be hospitalized. Do not get me wrong. Hospitalization is often needed. But this is where a chaplain must be involved. He must engage and have a fight in the battle, the spiritual battle. He also must communicate with the doctors because a drugged patient who is incoherent cannot come out of darkness. The doctor is simply sedating a veteran in captivity. There must be balance. All the veteran's types of wounds must be treated simultaneously. The chaplain deliberately needs to communicate that the veteran has spiritual wounds that they need treatment for those wounds as well. For military chaplains who are reading this, fight the good fight!

Veterans Administration Intervention

Veterans crisis line at *1-800-273-8255* and *press 1*, send a text message to *838255*.

All veterans have had issues with the Veterans Administration. In most cases, I still try to give them the benefit of the doubt, and they are still part of my health care. They are for many veterans. There are many other veterans who, through true horror stories, misinformation, malpractice, mistreatment, and grown distrust, do not use Veterans Administration services.

The Veterans Administration has also struggled significantly with the issue of suicide. But they are moving in the right direction. The "VA believes that everyone has a role to play in preventing suicide. That's why we are working with community partners across the country—including faith communities, employers, schools, and health care organizations—to prevent suicide among **all** Veterans, including those who may never come to VA for care."[3] It is a great sign that they are recognizing that they alone are not enough. They have also been beat up quite a bit about suicide rates and what they are doing about it. It really is not fair to them. Everyone really does have a role. It is our role in ministry to work with the VA to attend to the spiritual wounds that veterans have. They have a lot of resources, and we can have a lot more success with the VA than fighting against them. Have the "one team, one fight" mentality.

Here is what the VA says about suicide:

The Veterans Administration lists warning signs of someone who is thinking about suicide:

- Hopelessness, feeling like there's no way out
- Anxiety, agitation, sleeplessness, or mood swings
- Feeling like there is no reason to live
- Rage or anger
- Engaging in risky activities without thinking
- Increasing alcohol or drug misuse
- Withdrawing from family and friends

Then they offer signs that require immediate attention:

- Thinking about hurting or killing yourself
- Looking for ways to kill yourself
- Talking about death, dying, or suicide
- Self-destructive behavior, such as drug misuse, carelessly handling weapons, etc.

At this point in your study, you see a lot of parallels to the issues of trauma. I like how the Veterans Administration explains that not all suicides are based on trauma. However, I focus on trauma because it is the leading issue I see among veterans in darkness. There simply are not enough studies being conducted on veteran suicides based on trau-

---

3 US Department of Veteran Affairs, https://www.mentalhealth.va.gov/suicide_prevention/.

matic events. It is an issue, I think, we need to tackle because a veteran's suicide for any reason other than trauma is nothing different than the civilian causes of suicide nationwide. If it were not for trauma, veteran suicides would be more in line with the national average. Suicide rates are higher in the military in times of war. Why? Trauma!

Serve Ministries Inc. is now a Veterans Administration endorsing agency. What that means is that we can endorse people to gain full-time employment as chaplains for the VA through our ministry. We compliment the training they get with our focus on crisis and trauma, our mentorship to get into the psychiatric wards to minister to the veterans through their different types of wounds within the Veterans Administration hospitals they are assigned. Our focus is to keep them grounded, minister to them, mentor them, and encourage them to remain assertive in their ministry with the foreknowledge that veterans will not come to them.

National Strategy for Preventing Veterans' Suicide

The National Strategy for Preventing Veterans Suicide states that "portrayals of Veteran suicide in the news and entertainment media too often perpetuate the misconception that a Veteran's suffering from mental trauma is always the result of combat exposure and that suicide cannot be prevented."[4] First, suicide is preventable with intervention and treatment, but the right types of treatment for the different types of wounds the veteran is facing. Second, although I do not disagree that all mental trauma is the result of combat exposure, a key element is missing. The reason why military suicide rates are higher is because they have a correlation to combat exposure. I do not believe in marginalizing the issue. The reason why the rates are higher are twofold:

1. Veterans are exposed to traumatic events.
2. We are not engaging with the veteran before they fall below the critical line into darkness and lose hope.

---

4 US Department of Veterans Affairs, Office of Mental Health and Suicide Prevention, National Strategy for Preventing Veteran Suicide 2018–2028, page 19.

The strategy also reports the following:

There is no single cause of suicide. Suicide deaths reflect a complex interaction of risk and protective factors at the individual, community, and societal levels. Risk factors are characteristics associated with a greater likelihood of suicidal behaviors. Some risk factors for suicide include the following:

- Prior suicide attempt(s).
- Mental health conditions.
- Stressful life events such as divorce, job loss, or the death of a loved one.
- Availability of lethal means protective factors can help offset risk factors.

These are characteristics associated with a lesser likelihood of suicidal behaviors. Some protective factors for suicide include the following:

- Positive coping skills
- Having reasons for living or a sense of purpose in life
- Feeling connected to other people
- Access to mental health care

In addition to the protective factors described above, veterans may possess unique protective factors related to their service, such as resilience or a strong sense of belonging to a unit. They may also possess risk factors related to their military service, such as service-related injury or a recent transition from military service to civilian life. Preventing veteran suicide requires strategies that maximize protective factors while minimizing risk factors at all levels throughout communities nationwide.[5]

I recommend reading the study because it is not a bad read. It is best to do additional research on your own and refer to chapter 4 for recommendations to help the veterans you administer to. One

[5] Ibid, 6.

final recommendation is to stay engaged with the veteran through the process of getting help with other professionals. There is a lot of pain the veteran is experiencing with all their wounds between appointment, while hospitalized, while at home, etc. You need to be his battle buddy!

Police/First Responders Intervention

Police stations, fire departments, EMS, and corrections officers at the local, state, and federal level are almost all independent organizations with no centralized response for suicide other than this:

The National Suicide Prevention lifeline: 1-800-273-8255

One important organization to get to know is Blue H.E.L.P. (Honor. Educate. Lead. Prevent.). Their mission is "offering comfort and honor to the families who have lost an officer to suicide is a necessary to maintain the credibility of the thin blue line. All officers, regardless of method of death, deserve thanks; all families deserve your support." The organization brings awareness, training, commitment to serve others, and free materials to give to police officers, firefighters, and EMS personnel.[6] I get materials from them, but putting up posters does not reach people. These resources only help if you as the chaplain are using them in your discussions.

The Solution

"Whoever is not with me is against me, and whoever does not gather with me scatters" (Matthew 12:30 ESV).

Now it is time for "the" solution. We need godly men and women to respond to their calling. God calls on many, and very few take actions and fulfill their true purpose in life. I find it rather disheartening, but I am also rather guilty of the same thing; we all are. I have fallen short many times when God has called on me. I have spent much time repenting over this. My responding has led to a conscious change in my behavior and has driven me to action. With

---

6 Blue H.E.L.P., https://bluehelp.org/resources/training-and-resources/.

renewed determination and a focus response to my calling, I now relentlessly pursue my God-given purpose to "serve with those who serve."[7]

I am a firm believer that God calls you to worship Him in everything you do. God does not just want you to attend church on Sunday. He wants a day-by-day, week-by-week, and year-by-year relationship and commitment to His will. What this also means is that you have experiences that are supposed to translate into ministry. I mentioned it before: it takes a veteran to heal a veteran, a police officer to heal a police officer, etc. But it is even more than that. Your belief in God, learning His word, your experiences, and your calling uniquely qualify you to minister to military and/or first responders.

You need to be the first responder by asserting yourself in someone's life held captive in darkness. It is a matter of life and death. If you know of a veteran or a first responder in this state, do not wait; go now! Stay engaged and realize you have backup. Call on them but remain engaged.

---

7 "Motto of Serve Ministries Inc.," https://ServeMinistriesInc.com.

Review/Application Questions

1. Where is the spiritual battleground, and what are the forces fighting in spiritual warfare?
2. Why does Satan fight against your soul once you have been saved?
3. You should never go it alone; can you list some other organizations at the national level (not mentioned) that can help you in your ministry?
4. What are the contributing factors that have veteran suicide rates higher than the national average, and where are we losing them at a higher rate than combat action?
5. What suggestions do you have for the VA to implement in order to address the issue of veterans' suicide?
6. What additional steps can first responder organizations/departments take to reduce suicide rates, which are higher than the rates we lose them in the line of duty?
7. What do you need to do in ministry to help someone captive in darkness?

CHAPTER 6

LIFE CONTAINS CRISIS

Therefore, we do not lose heart. Though outwardly we are wasting away, yet inwardly we are being renewed day by day. For our light and momentary troubles are achieving for us an eternal glory that far outweighs them all. So, we fix our eyes not on what is seen, but on what is unseen, since what is seen is temporary, but what is unseen is eternal.

—2 Corinthians 4:16–18 NIV

Nobody in life will escape crisis if you live into adulthood. We will all experience some degree of a crisis situation whether it is a loss of a job, death of a friend or family member, divorce, financial devastation, severe health issues, retirement transition, a natural disaster, an accident, and more. At the time of writing this book, the world is going through a global COVID-19 pandemic crisis that has cost over one hundred thousand lives and billions of dollars. Jobs have been lost, hourly wage workers are struggling to make ends meet, and there are many combat health issues as they recover. Some crisis situations can be personal matters while others can be major events that happen around you such as a plane crash, a murder in your town, and unexpected suicide of someone close to you, a horrible accident, a forest fire, a tornado, or a factory shutdown. As you can tell, nobody escapes being faced with a crisis.

Definition of Crisis

A definition of a *crisis* is "a period of psychological disequilibrium, experienced as a result of an event or situation that constitutes a significant problem that cannot be remedied by the use of familiar coping strategies."[8] A crisis is when it becomes insurmountable to handle what occurred and it impacts the person's quality of life. We see crisis events happen all around us when we watch the news, hear stories from others, and see the impacts they have on people. They can feel depressed, helpless, guilty, exhausted, and it can cause severe anxiety.[9]

Crisis is quite different than trauma. I have read many books and articles where those lines are blurred. To put this in perspective, I was part of a unit where a fellow soldier committed suicide. His roommate walked in on him and found him. It was very graphic from what he told me, and he could not get the images out of his head. He saw his face, and he saw the blood. He experienced a traumatic event. For me and the rest of the unit, it was a crisis. We had someone we all knew take his life. He was no longer with us, and it impacted the unit. Although it was a crisis in our unit, we did not suffer the trauma that my fellow soldier had to deal with by seeing the dead body. This chapter focuses on crisis because there is a different way to minister to crisis situations than to trauma.

Elements of a Crisis

There are four major elements to a crisis:

- The event that leads to or causes a crisis
- The emotional reaction to the event

---

[8] Goff, Doyle R. PhD, "Ministering to People in Crisis," Ministerial Internship Program Seminar IV.

[9] Ibid.

- The inability to make sense of what happened
- Being emotionally debilitated from the event

When all four components come together, you have a crisis.[10] Some people handle crisis situations better than others. Therefore, to minister to someone in crisis, you must take time to listen and understand what they are saying. Do not try to define their emotion for them or provide a solution. Do not minimalize the situation even if you do not think it is not a big deal; it apparently is to them. Compassion goes a long way, and many times being that is the first step to helping them cope. But this is also a time for assessment: is the person showing all four elements?

"Count it all joy, my brothers, when you meet trials of various kinds, for you know that the testing of your faith produces steadfastness. And let steadfastness have its full effect, that you may be perfect and complete, lacking in nothing" (James 1:2–4 NIV).

Ministering to Someone in Crisis

There are some positive things you can do to assist someone in their time of crisis:

- Form prayer teams and action teams in your local church.
- Take the person to a doctor's appointment, especially if the person communicates that they are scared or reluctant about going.
- Visit them if they are in the hospital.
- Provide food to their family. Many churches are exceptionally good at this.
- Assist with small children by providing or helping coordinate childcare.
- Provide materials and/or offer to do small home repairs or lawn maintenance.

---

10 Ibid.

- Remember that you are not there to judge. Do not focus on the event; focus on the person. Listen![11]
- Be patient and compassionate.
- Communicate needs to those who can help and provide updates.

Preparation before a crisis is also important. I encourage everyone to use their local church. A chaplain can help the local church with establishing prayer teams and action teams. Our ministry has people focused on ministering to people, but we leverage resources in the community. The most important resource, by God's design, is the local church. Plus, they are an incredibly good source of godly manpower. It is relatively easy to pull together "prayer warriors" to form a prayer team when needed. It is a little more challenging, but very doable, to form action teams that can provide food, transportation, limited financial support (benevolence funds), childcare, etc.[12] To formulate these teams, it is best to pull in church leaders to gain their support and remind people of their calling as Christians.

"Therefore, my dear brothers and sisters, stand firm. Let nothing move you. Always give yourselves fully to the work of the Lord because you know that your labor in the Lord is not in vain" (1 Corinthians 15:58 NIV).

Crisis Intervention

The word *crisis* is largely overused and watered down in our language. Someone who is upset over something can say that they are having a crisis because they had an argument with someone, had a flat tire, tore their favorite shirt, misplaced their car keys, etc. But this is not a real crisis. A person who is experiencing a real crisis needs someone to intervene. They are experiencing all four elements previously mentioned. Crisis intervention may be needed after you have had time to learn and understand the crisis the person is going

---

[11] Herring, Jerri, "Ministering in Time of Crisis," Leadership Lesson 27.

[12] Ibid.

through by counseling them. I am not talking about professional psychological counseling; I am talking about ministerial counseling. The other may also be necessary, but in ministry, we provide that "front line" ministerial counseling. Dr. Norman Wright suggests examining Jesus's approach to counseling[13]:

- Acceptance: Jesus accepted them as they were and then worked with them realizing their potential.
- Discernment: Jesus directly assessed and then addressed their immediate needs.
- Emphasized right behavior: he was extremely interested in them going forward and not sinning.
- Assisted people in accepting responsibility: he placed the responsibility and decision for a person to make a change on the individual.
- Hope: Jesus gave hope that all things were possible through Him.
- Encouragement: Jesus encouraged the people He ministered to.
- Peace of mind: Jesus provided people with the reality of peace and hope.
- Teaching: Jesus used teachings as part of His counseling.

There are many models on crisis intervention that exist. The most common and widely accepted model is from Dr. Albert Roberts, who developed a seven-step model to crisis intervention[14]:

1. Conduct a safety assessment.

    - Is this a 911 call for the police or for an ambulance?

---

[13] Wright, Norman. 1985. *Crisis Intervention.* San Bernardino: Here's Life Publishers Inc.

[14] Roberts, Albert R. 1991. *Contemporary Perspectives on Crisis Intervention and Prevention.* Englewood Cliffs: Prentice Hall.

- Is there a risk to their safety or to the safety of someone else?

2. Establish effective communication.
3. Identify immediate and major issues.
4. Understand their feelings and provide encouragement.
5. Explore alternatives.
6. Develop a plan of action.

    - Identify additional people or organizations to support.
    - Provide coping recommendations.
    - Refer for professional counseling.
    - Encourage positive/measurable actions.

7. Follow up.

I highly recommend Dr. Robert's book *Contemporary Perspectives on Crisis Intervention and Prevention* for more information and greater understanding. I will not create my own model in this area. However, people in crisis need the following: safety, security (privacy), ventilation (express their feeling), validation (acknowledgment), prediction (what will happen next), and preparation (how to physically and emotionally move forward).[15] Preparation is key, so developing your own plan of action to conduct a crisis intervention is necessary for ministry.

"Do not merely look out for your own personal interests, but also for the interests of others" (Philippians 2:4 NIV).

Ministering to Those who Serve

The focus of Serve Ministries Inc. (SMI) is to train and equip chaplains to minister to those who serve. Our motto is to "serve with

[15] Flesburg, Evon O. 2008. "Ministering to People in Crisis: Don't Just Stand There!" Preaching in the Moment (Aug/Sept/Oct 2008) issue of *Circuit Rider*.

those who serve," and those who serve need to be ministered to as well. We often cite 1 Corinthians 15:58, which is also on our logo. But let us look closer on what God says about responding to others in their time of need. We will use the biblical story of the death of Lazarus and how Jesus ministered during a time of crisis. Read the death of Lazarus in your Bible (John 11:1–45).

Let us examine these verses further on what Jesus did[16]:

Verses 1–2: Jesus responded in a time of need
Verses 3–5: Jesus responded in love
Verses 4–7: Jesus responded when others did not understand
Verse 8: Jesus responded even during difficulties
Verses 9–10: Jesus responded to the opportunity to serve
Verses 11–15: Jesus responded when others did not understand His intensions
Verses 20–21 and 36: Jesus responded even when He was criticized
Verses 22–26: Jesus responded to provide hope and comfort
Verses 33–36: Jesus responded when they grieved and wept
Verse 37: Jesus responded when he was falsely judged
Verses 38–40 Jesus responded with compassion and did what he could
Versus 40–45: Jesus responded to bring life out of death

Responding to a crisis is difficult and will come with many challenges. Jesus still responded during all the challenges that were previously mentioned. The key is, he still responded. We are expected to respond as well, even in the face of many challenges. Far too often, we expect our service to God to go without challenges. He makes no promises to that. If Jesus faced challenges, so will you. Your greatest challenge will be if you still choose to respond.

[16] List derived from an article presented by Kellie Van Guilder titled "Chaplains Join NC Community in Honoring Fallen Police Officer" provided by the Billy Graham response team, May 9, 2019.

Responding to Disaster

Responding to a disaster is even more complex than responding to an individual in crisis. In a disaster, you are responding to multiple individuals in crisis, and you will not be able to minister to everyone. Therefore, you will not be able to minister alone. You need help with additional manpower and resources. You must choose how you are going to minister and to whom. You will need to shape what you will do when you get there, so you must have a plan.

Here are five key things to remember when you are developing your disaster plan[17]:

1. The best time to prepare is before a disaster. Develop a plan before getting involved in disaster relief/ministry.
2. Monetary donations are more important than more volunteers:

    - $10—can feed someone probably for the day
    - $30—can provide supplies needed for cleanup
    - $100—can provide snack and drinks to over one hundred survivors
    - $250—can provide hot meals and a water station to one hundred people for twenty-four hours
    - $500—can provide a Salvation Army mobile feeding unit for a day

3. The best way to provide monetary support is through an established relief agency.

    - They are well equipped to support the masses.
    - Great place for people to volunteer with a focused purpose and/or provide financial support to get the biggest "bang for the buck."

[17] Stetzer, Ed. 2017. "5 Ways to Get Involved in Disaster Relief."

4. By giving to agencies in place, you minimize inefficiencies and get resources to identified areas of need.
5. Avoid the temptation to load up a truckful of stuff and just go.

    - Delivering old furniture, used clothes, used supplies, and perishable food creates more junk piles in a disaster area.
    - Unsolicited donations are not always helpful and not always wanted. This leads to frustration to both the giver and the receiver.
    - Best to communicate with organizations that have identified needs and sign up to deliver what is needed to a specific drop-off point.

I will add another important note to this list. *Your focus is to help people in need by addressing their immediate need and show them you care and that Jesus loves them. You are not there to take advantage of the situation to go on an evangelical crusade.* I know this is a controversial topic, but I go back to the example of Jesus in His ministry. In times of crisis, He addressed the need before giving His message. You need to address the needs before you give His message. When people cannot thank you enough for all the love and support you give them, then you can share the message of Christ because it is a message of hope and strength. People will be saved from this experience; they always are. But there is a time for it, after their immediate needs are being met. One of the worst things I have seen is someone going to just pray with people empty-handed. If it were me, I would hand those Christians a chainsaw first. Go there to serve, not just to pray.

Recommendation for Application

To me, the most important part of your plan needs to be, Who are you ministering to? The answer cannot be anyone and everyone God puts in your path. I have heard many Christians say this, and they all mean well. But it is far greater of a task than you can handle.

Certainly, you may be faced with someone who needs immediate help, and you will feel the Holy Spirit tell you to do something, and you will. But you must have a ministry mission that is focused on something more than just showing up and winging it.

For me, it is ministering to first responders in a time of a natural disaster. At the time of this writing, it is the Niceville Police Department. If they are not involved, then I would latch on to a first responder organization, that is. There are many other church organizations, Christian relief organizations, and individual Christians crawling through a disaster area. My focus is on those who are serving. My plan is focused on them. Everything else is secondary. I certainly can bring supplies with me for another relief organization. But my plan focuses on asking first responders what they need me to bring. It provides focus on where I go, when I get there, and who specifically I will dedicate my efforts. I spend my resources on precisely what is needed. When I get it, I know exactly who I am delivering it to.

First responders will be working long hours experiencing physical and emotional fatigue. They will see many things and feel the effects of the crisis. Many may have even been impacted by the crisis and are trying to do their job while also being worried about their family. They will be under immense stress, and they will get wounded from it. You will too!

> "Come to me, all who labor and are heavy laden, and I will give you rest. Take my yoke upon you, and learn from me, for I am gentle and lowly in heart, and you will find rest for your souls. For my yoke is easy, and my burden is light." (Matthew 11:28–30 NIV)

Focus on the "pulse" of the officers who are physically injured, psychologically/emotionally injured, socially injured, and spiritually injured. That is right! All four types of wounds. This may consist of telling them to get minor physical wounds treated so it does not get infected, even if you must be adamant about it, even if it means you pulling out your Neosporin and bandages to do it on the spot.

If their hand gets infected by a cut, they will not be useful in the long run. They must rest, eat, hydrate, shower, and recuperate before going out each time. Many officers will become emotional and show signs that the crisis is having a psychological impact. They will see so much devastation and loss of life that it can be overwhelming. Socially, they could have issues with their families because they are gone so much and especially if their families were impacted by the disaster too. They will also have spiritual challenges just like everyone else, wondering, *Where was God when all this happened?* or *Why did He allow this to happen?*

Again, it does not mean you should not help someone else in need. When presented with an immediate need, I will help. But I will turn them over to someone else in ministry or to a service at my first opportunity. My focus is on my officers as part of my plan. That way, every day I go out, I know precisely where I am going, what I am bringing for them, who I am talking to, who I am praying with, and it allows others to expect and rely on me.

Ministering during a natural disaster is also a marathon, not a sprint. Hurricane Michael hit Northwest Florida in 2018. Two weeks after the hurricane, those who still had homes, churches, and businesses did not have water or electricity. A year later, many were still living in trailers or moved out of town. The hurricane will take years to recover from.[18] As chaplains, we will need to be prepared that your first responders will be operating in a damaged area for years, and you may be ministering to the wounds of this disaster for the duration of your time as a chaplain. Hurricane Katrina happened in 2005. A study a year later showed that government response was slow and had resource constraints, poor leadership, weak planning, poor communication, and limited training. People were outraged and suffering. First responders were overwhelmed. The report said that even if we learned these lessons, the next generation would have to learn them

[18] Colson, Margaret. 2019. "Hurricane Michael: One Year Later," second in a series of stories on the first anniversary of Hurricane Michael.

again.[19] I personally think that is simply an operational environment you can expect.

There is a compounding issue when a first responder is worried about his/her family; being conflicted on where they should really be is challenging. It is one thing to say "duty calls," but it is something else to know that you are not there for your family when they need you most. This can be rather overwhelming, and their family may not be so forgiving. They can be even less forgiving in times of disaster when they are impacted, and the officer has those "duty calls" moments. Family stress compounded with occupational stress is difficult, especially when the officer on top of all that starts exhibiting compounding wounds.

Most of us remember the horrible effects of the terrorist attacks on September 11, 2001. John Delendick was a fire department chaplain in New York. He lost a fellow chaplain Mychal Judge and many firemen when the first tower collapsed. He remembered the hardest thing that day was when people asked him if he had seen their friends and family members and struggling how to respond to their desperate pleas. He visited the rubble for months afterward, accompanying family members to search for loved ones. For a year after, he could not recall how many funerals and memorial services he attended.[20] At the Pentagon, chaplains tried to minister to military and first responders. Army Chaplain COL Timothy Mallard recalls trying to talk to first responders, "You talk about feeling overwhelmed and inadequate. I was trying to get them to share their experiences and concerns and fears, but there was still a point where I feel like I just wasn't connecting." So he pulled out a Bible and read Psalm 23. "When I got to the point in that Psalm where David says walk through the valley of the shadow of death, I looked to my right at the building. There was just this black gaping hole." When he finished with the reading,

---

[19] Goodrick, Jake; Waltimore, Bridgette, Anderson, Natalie; Gravius, Christian. 2019. "'Everyone is a First responder' in Disasters, Police and Firefighter Say." News 21.

[20] Escobar, Allyson. 2019. "Memories of 9/11 Attacks Linger for Former Fire Department Chaplain."

they locked arms and prayed. Then they said, "Okay, Chaplain, now we're ready." And they went back in. He remembers going back to the chaplain's tent and broke down crying.[21]

"Even though I walk through the valley of the shadow of death, I fear no evil, for You are with me; Your rod and Your staff, they comfort me" (Psalm 23:4 NIV).

Ministering to First Responders

Ministering to the first responders is a real need. As previously stated, when crisis strikes, first responders answer the call to prevent or mitigate human suffering and loss of life. Each case only builds on the previous one. First responders will expose themselves and even risk their lives for others. The more they are exposed, they tend to experience increased anxiety, sadness, post-traumatic symptoms, anger, depression, physical and mental exhaustion, and even alcohol abuse. We categorized those as wounds. No matter how people relabel them or what symptoms they experience, you can bend them in the four types of wounds that we covered. It does not happen just during natural disaster; it happens with simply serving in the line of duty.

I am incredibly grateful for the following illustrations provided by Investigator Lee. Many of these were extremely difficult for him to share, but he felt moved by God to give people a perspective of the life of a police officer facing crisis and trauma and the need for ministry:

[21] Panzino, Charlsy. 2018. "Chaplains Reunite 16 Years after 9/11 Attack on the Pentagon."

Officer Down

I was in my office working on paperwork in the middle of the day. It was relayed that an officer had been shot in the head in the town twenty minutes over. The shooter was being chased into my city jurisdiction. All of my department was mobilized. The shooter drove into a local hotel and barricaded himself inside a second-floor room. I took an inner perimeter position approximately thirty yards from the shooter's room. I was around the corner of the bend standing guard with the SWAT team robot operator who was recording the shooter's doorway. I viewed the shooter walk out of the room and confront the SWAT team who responded by shooting him multiple times. I held the stairway door open for the SWAT team as they carried the shooter downstairs to the awaiting ambulance.

What I saw on the robot video did not affect me. The smell of gunpowder, the multiple sounds of shots fired, even when I made eye contact with the shooter being carried by with gunshots did not affect me. The single droplet of blood I found on the collar of my yellow button-up shirt did not seem to affect me. What affected me was losing the officer who was shot in the head. He was one of my mentors when I started down the path of becoming a cop in 1995. He had been one of my mentors for nearly twenty years. I am not over losing him. God helps me move forward. RIP, Bill.

Ministering to first responders must be deliberate. Most are highly motivated, altruistic, fearless, and so highly driven that they often overlook taking care of themselves.[22] When the going gets tough, they work harder and longer. For those who are rescuing victims, they can be overwhelmed quickly. Imagine trying to save someone's life after a car accident and you are unsuccessful, and they die right before you. Imagine more than one needing saving from a burning house, and you are unable to save them all. They will keep that inside and show strength. But when alone and they have time to decompress, the gravity of the situation kicks in.

[22] Pfeffer, Kendall; Buser, Sam, PhD; and Tran, Jana, PhD. 2018. "Disaster Mental Health: Meeting the Unique Needs of First Responders."

I think one of the hardest times for officers is when they lose someone in the line of duty they knew. They can go on an emotional rollercoaster from crying to anger to depression to frustration. They will also go through moments where they stand in a daze while time passes, not realizing they are not moving or not knowing what they were supposed to be doing. Let us read about another one of Investigator Lee's stories. When you read it, think about where he is at in the H3 cycle and what wounds he may be experiencing. How would you minister to him?

SWAT Officer Down

I was a patrol shift corporal when I received a court order to take a man into custody and deliver him to a receiving facility for a mental evaluation. A yellow sticky was stuck to the top of the court order with a handwritten note that read, "He owns a shotgun and has said he will kill the police." My patrol lieutenant and a shift officer accompanied me over to the address. I circled the house to take up a position in the rear of the home. When I got to the back corner of the home, I saw the man playing with his dog in the backyard. It looked as if he had shaved his head with scissors. Judging by his appearance alone, I believed it would be difficult to have a rational conversation. I showed him the court order and tried to explain that his family was worried about him. He started getting hostile quickly. We handcuffed him for safety. We nearly had to carry him to the patrol car. I followed the shift officer who dove the man to the receiving facility. At the facility personnel's request, we escorted the man into the holding cell. I took the handcuffs off him and backed out of the cell while he was aggressively coming at me. I was able to make it out safely and closed the door.

Sometime during the day, the receiving facility for mental evaluations transferred the man to the local hospital to be mentally evaluated. The man walked out of the emergency room and escaped. Two of the shift officers in my unit located him running barefoot behind a business near the hospital. He fought them. He was secured and placed in the back of a patrol car. He kicked out the back window with his bare feet, causing lacerations. He was successfully transported back to the hospital for mental evaluation and injury treatment.

The next morning at around 4:00 a.m., I was called into work. The man had escaped the hospital again. This time, the hospital allegedly did not report his escape for nearly three hours, giving him enough time to make it back to his parent's empty home. He had barricaded himself inside the home and would not respond to anyone. I drove to the command post a few houses down. I provided as much detail as possible to the SWAT commander concerning my interactions with the man. The SWAT commander made the decision to enter the home to recapture the mental evaluation escapee.

The SWAT team stacked up and prepared to march toward the target residence. This was my old team. These guys were my team. The team made entry into the home and discovered every door in the home was closed. The call was made for a slow methodical search room by room. The last door was breached, and the lead operator was struck by shotgun blast. The number 2 man stepped up and laced the gunman with his assigned MP5. The third man in the stack was able to drag the point man back to the team medic. The gunman was able to turn his shotgun on himself and ended his life.

EMS was called and was approximately fifteen minutes out. When EMS finally arrived, the SWAT member was loaded into the ambulance. I led the ambulance with my patrol car, lights and sirens blaring. The reality of what had occurred had not set in. We got to the emergency room, the same emergency room where the man had escaped. I helped pull the SWAT operator out of the ambulance. His right boot and sock were off, so the paramedic could check his pulse. His upper torso was covered in blood. He took a shotgun blast about an inch above his tactical vest line in the lower throat area. We wheeled him into the emergency room where the doctors immediately started working on him. I stood there in the doorway holding his bloody guns while they did everything they could to save his life. A nurse came up and asked if the escaped mental evaluation shot him. I said yes.

I delivered his bloody guns to the SWAT team leader. The state was on scene investigating the shooting inside the home. I was standing there, in front of the house, next to my sergeant when we got the call from the emergency room. They could not save him.

I grew up with an abusive alcoholic father. I was taught early on that emotions are weak, and men do not cry. This day changed me. I started crying on my sergeant's shoulder and had a hard time stopping. Something in me clicked. Duty before self.

It was my shift covering patrol, and I had to lead my guys who were just as distraught as I was. While I was standing there, with his blood on my uniform from his guns, dispatch called my number. I was dispatched to a natural death. Duty before self. I pulled up to the address and had to console a forty-eight-year-old man because his sixty-eight-year-old mother had died from her many illnesses overnight. Duty before self. I went into autopilot and followed orders to serve my community.

For the next two weeks, I could only function in uniform. I could not pray. I could not make any decisions. I would stand up from the couch, take two steps, and forget what I was going to do. I would sit back down. In uniform, I functioned as I should. Out of uniform, I was crashing. I could not pray; my mind would not allow me to complete a thought. I was on the honorary motor unit. It was an ancillary position mostly using the department motorcycles for parades. I was assigned to guard and escort our fallen officer on his final day before he was laid to rest. Most of these memories are a blur.

I found myself standing in my kitchen. I do not recall how I got there or how long I stood there. I was just there. My wife appeared in front of me. Up until this moment, she gave me space. She did not know how to reach me, so she thought it best to let me find my way back. I broke down and cried on her shoulder in my kitchen for what seemed like days. I needed help. I could not come back on my own. This fallen officer was not only my SWAT brother, he was my friend. I drove to my department looking for a chaplain. The human resource manager met me first and said, "Oh, we forgot you were there too." My chosen chaplain was not there, so I met with the new guy. I told him I still could not pray, and I was not getting better. He let me talk, and we cried together. And then we prayed together. I had never been so happy in my life to talk to God. I felt like he had abandoned me.

I felt like he would not hear my cries. I have never felt so alone. That moment, I knew God did not abandon me. My remorse, my self-placed guilt, my inability to understand my emotions, my inability to reach out for help, my self-isolation, my…my…my…

The next several years were challenging. The motor unit I was assigned to was to escort the family of our beloved fallen SWAT officer to the state capitol and to Washington, DC, for police week. I joined a group of law enforcement officers from around the state and rode the *Tour de Force*, which was an organized charity bike ride from Miami to Daytona Beach in his name. We presented checks to the family. I was interviewed in detail by the state for my rolls in what built up to the officer involved shooting.

It has taken several years to "get better". Through God and the unyielding help from my wife, I have found my way back. I will never be who I was, but I am functioning "better".

The need for chaplains in first responder organization is way understated. I am appalled by the number of first responder organizations that do not have a chaplain, especially with what we see happening in our nation today. For those that have volunteers, I am surprised that they do not budget for a full-time chaplain. A first responder organization needs a full-time paid chaplain. For smaller organizations, a city could probably bring on a chaplain to cover all their first responder organizations (police, fire, and EMS) in the area. But I still highly recommend a professional chaplain. They can be augmented by volunteer chaplains, but this is full-time ministry work.

Ministering to first responders is challenging. Probably the greatest challenge is the need to be assertive in someone's life, but that requires trust. You must have a "ministry of presence," which is extremely difficult for a volunteer. If you are a volunteer, do your best.

Here are some recommendations for chaplains to prepare for crisis events in your departments:

- Get to know everyone in the department. Takes notes on the side. It helps in follow-up so they do not have to always answer the same question twice. Personally, I study my notes so I can remember names and follow up on issues. It shows I care, but there is no way we can remember everything. I am horrible at names unless I make a conscious effort to remember. Notes is the best way, but nobody will ever see my notes.

- Note family members' names, ages of children, pets.
- Spouse's occupation.
- Interest outside of work.

- Get everyone's contact information (phone and email).
- Occupational experience—are they new to the department, fresh out of the academy, or have they been doing this for twenty-five years?
- Show interest in their job. Ask questions especially if it is not your background. I was in the army for twenty-seven years and became the Niceville Police Department chaplain. I have never been a police officer before. I was upfront about it and said, "I will ask questions that you guys probably think is common knowledge. Help me learn, and it will be common knowledge to me too."
- Participate: If they let you do training, try to do it, and take it seriously. Give your best, and they will respect you for trying. Joke around like I have seen others do, and you will be a distraction.
- Spend time with them on the duty day. This allows you to start ministering to them when they are doing their day-to-day activities. You do not want to wait for a crisis to occur before you do all the above.
- When a crisis occurs, focus on them.
- Most crisis situations you will encounter will be limited to a small audience. Find out all officers involved and focus on each of them individually.
- Have a plan for natural disasters, even if it is only a one-page plan.

- Does the department have a natural disaster plan? If so, get a copy.
- Do they train for natural disasters? If so, try to attend.
- Who do they leverage and connect with? Do they have chaplains? If so, meet and get to know them.
- Share your plan with your chief.

- Identify other ministries, churches, and organization in your area that would help in time of a natural disaster.

Christ-focused ministry is a must, but it is not about a denominational viewpoint or about a personal belief. This is what I call the "truths of Christ" that are essential to be a Christian. You know what they are, so I will not expound on them here. At all costs, I avoid theological debates and only focus on the "truths" about Christ. If someone wants to discuss a theological topic, I try to cover it from multiple angles and what some of the most common views are. This is important because we are there to establish rapport, and theological debates can cause division. If it really gets pressing, offer to study the topic with them further. When an officer experiences a crisis or is suffering from the effects of dealing with a crisis, it is not a time to be evangelical. It is a time to help them with their need, offer godly counsel, pray with them, speak with them, and help them to get back to a normal state so they can continue to do their job.

I do not evangelize as a chaplain. I have met many who do, but I adamantly do not. People will "open up" one-on-one and want to talk about Christ because they know I am the chaplain, and when I am able to, I share how Christ has worked in my life. There will be an appropriate time to ask them if they know Jesus. If they do, I believe them and speak to them as a Christian regardless of their denomination or how they have been baptized. If they are not, then I will talk to them a while about it. When they show interest, then I will share the "good news" with them. That is Holy Spirit-led, not me-led. I know this is controversial too. I have had others tell me, "What if they go on a 911 call within the next few minutes, and they lose their life in the line of duty and they did not know Christ?" Valid point! But I have never led anyone to Christ by shoving it down their throat either, and in my over thirty years' experience being around chaplains, I do not find very many successful chaplains if they are about evangelism first. It is all about timing. Do not lead off with it when you are meeting an officer, and do not do it while they are suffering from wounds when they need help. Only exception to the rule is if they are dying. Use sound judgment!

My last recommendation during a crisis is not to be a part of the crisis. For instance, I once responded to the scene of a baby drowning. The police officer who first responded was clearly emotional about it. You read about this story in a previous chapter. The paramedics appeared also disturbed by the scene. For some reason, it is natural to want to go and look at what happened. I refused that temptation. It is important to guard yourself. After all, that is not what I am there for. I am there to be a chaplain to the officer. My place on the scene is to talk to the first officer on the scene when his work is done and all the other officers and first responders involved. I attend any debriefing, and I assertively follow up. I protect myself from having to deal with the effect of the crisis so I can do my part, which is ministry.

Ministering to Veterans in Crisis

This could probably be a separate book or at least a separate chapter. Here we will briefly discuss veterans dealing with crisis. Furthermore, we will be only discussing veterans who have separated or retired from the military. When I run into someone on active status, I may minister to them briefly but will often refer them to a military chaplain to work with them on their crisis. There are only a few whom I minister to on active duty only by their request and only because they have told me that they think of me as a mentor.

It is very tragic what I am seeing happen to many veterans. It pains my heart beyond words. Many veterans leave the military with many wounds that becomes what I call *crisis no. 1*. They are still suffering from the effects of unmet needs where they are still suffering from different types of wounds. Now they leave the service, and they are personally in unchartered territory. If wounds were not being addressed before when services were readily available, they are unlikely being met now when resources become less available. You already know how to minister to the types of wounds, so you know how to deal with this crisis.

Crisis no. 2 is almost always an identity crisis when someone separates or retires from the military. They rose through the ranks, gained authority and prestige, increased responsibility, were valued and respected, and then in an instant, it was gone. I have talked with many veterans who actually looked forward to retirement, counted down the days, and secured a new job. Their family was completely looking forward to it, and you would think that there would not be an issue. But that veteran still ends up having an identity crisis when reality hits. They struggle with the adjustment and struggle with who they are now. The crisis is exponentially worse when the veteran is separate or retired against their will. They wanted to remain on active duty, and now it was stripped from them. This crisis is one where they had their identity taken away from them, and most feel lost when this happens.

The number 1 question I ask someone experiencing an identity crisis is, Who are you? I had a friend help me with then when I retired from the Army, and he asked me this question. Most will start talking about who they were. It is important to then help them through redefining who they are now. You cannot give them that answer as much as I have heard so many chaplains and ministers rush to the "you're a child of God" answer when it comes to your identity. It is more important that you lead them to the answer. That includes being a child of God and the environment around them (spouse, parent, etc.). When you help them to that conclusion, when they can acknowledge it, and when they have fully accepted it, then and only then do they own it. A person owns their identity, and they must own their new identity. I was forced to retire after twenty-seven years as a 100 percent disabled veteran; I did not want to retire. I wanted to make colonel, and I felt I had a good shot. I was a Christian, a seminary graduate, served in churches and ministries for many years, secured a job right away as a contractor on base, and I still had an identity crisis. One thing I did to help me was to not use lieutenant colonel (retired) as part of my identity. I also used my contractor ID to go on base instead of my retired military ID card so people would stop saluting me. I needed time to break away from that identity as I was redefining it. Those couple of things helped me.

Crisis no. 3 happens to every veteran the more disconnected they get from the military over time. They miss the comradery, the uniform, the serving, the assignments, and even the deployments. The realization for many leads to significant depression where it becomes a crisis. Many do not get the same satisfaction in the civilian world or the same level of responsibility, feel the same levels of importance, or even feel they are even relevant in the workplace anymore. This is where support groups, church veteran small groups, hobbies with other veterans, veterans' organizations, and ministry to other veterans can help the veteran have that increased sense of purpose. As a chaplain, helping someone "see" their God-given purpose is essential. We all have purpose through God, and sometimes, we just need help seeing it.

After that, crisis events will occur, and they are pretty much the same as anyone else going through a crisis. What you will want to be cognizant of are the wounds of a veteran. If they are hurting and if they are not healing, it can turn into a crisis. Not having purpose (the helping) can turn into a crisis. So do not forget the H3 cycle.

Biblical Reflection

"Therefore, I tell you, do not be anxious about your life, what you will eat or what you will drink, nor about your body, what you will put on. Is not life more than food, and the body more than clothing? Look at the birds of the air: they neither sow nor reap nor gather into barns, and yet your heavenly father feeds them. Are you not of more value than they? And which of you by being anxious can add a single hour to his span of life? And why are you anxious about clothing? Consider the lilies of the field, how they grow: they neither toil nor spin, yet I tell you, even Solomon in all his glory was not arrayed like one of these. But if God so clothes the grass of the field, which today is alive and tomorrow is thrown into the oven, will he not much more clothe you, O you of little faith? Therefore, do not be anxious, saying, 'What shall we eat?' or 'What shall we drink?' or 'What shall we wear?' For the Gentiles seek after all these things, and your heavenly father knows that you need them all. But seek first the kingdom of God and his righteousness, and all these things will be added to you. Therefore, do not be anxious about tomorrow, for tomorrow will be anxious for itself. Sufficient for the day is its own trouble" (Matthew 6:25–34 NIV).

Review Questions

1. What are the four elements of a crisis?
2. What are some positive things you can do to minister to someone in crisis? Is there anything you would add to the list?
3. What is Jesus's approach to counseling?
4. Why is developing a plan of action important for crisis intervention?
5. Jesus responded in times of crisis. If Jesus faced challenges, so will _____. Your greatest challenge will be if you still _______ _____ ________.
6. Summarize the things you need to consider in your disaster plan.
7. What are some things you learned about for a chaplain to be prepared for a crisis within the department? Is there something you would add?

CHAPTER 

IDENTITY: WHO ARE YOU?

So, in Christ Jesus you are all children of God through faith, for all of you who were baptized into Christ have clothed yourselves with Christ. There is neither Jew nor Gentile, neither slave nor free, nor is there male and female, for you are all one in Christ Jesus.

—Galatians 3:26–28

In the last chapter, we discussed that an identity crisis will occur when someone separates or retires from the military. The same is true for first responders. Whether you go through basic training, an academy, an officer's candidate school, or any related initial training, it starts an indoctrination process into a new culture. You learn new acronyms, and you are trained how to wear your uniform and how to perform your mission, and you begin a transformation from the person you were to the person you will become.

Once transformed, this new occupation becomes a large part of your identity. You spend most of your day at it. You are shaped by the experiences you encounter, and you develop social groups inside that culture. Your language changes, your values become refined, and you begin to unknowingly distance yourself from society mainstream. You become set apart and held to a different standard. You live under stricter rules and expectation on how you live your life. Your family adjusts to it as well the best they can. It is just reality!

Christians are not immune to an identity crisis either. They know they are children of God, but they end up still having an identity crisis when they leave public service. Why? It is because we spend more time identifying with what we do than we do on who we are. What we do becomes who we are. Think about it when you meet someone new. Typically, you start off introducing yourselves to get to know the other person's name. Then the question that usually follows is, What do you do? Our culture defines your identity based on what you do in society. It shapes your immediate impression with someone. When someone says, "I am Captain Kenneth Coburn, and I command an aircraft carrier," that tells you a lot about the person right there, and then follow-on questions may continue with that topic. How about, "My name is John Williams, and I am a New York firefighter." A New York firefighter also comes with an identity. Does that not immediately want you to ask if he was there on 9/11 and whether he knew firemen who lost their lives in one of the Twin Towers? You automatically shape your opinion of someone by what they do. It is exceedingly difficult to meet someone new without "what you do" coming into the conversation. It is what they will remember you by even if they do not remember your name.

If everyone you know besides your immediate family identifies you as a fireman, a police officer, a Marine, a general in the Army, a chief in the Navy, etc., separating/retiring from that profession causes a dilemma with your identity. I have met many Christians who will say that their service does not define them before they get out but then still experience an identity crisis when they do. I feel it is inevitable. The more prepared for life after service and the more retirement or separation is voluntary, the easier it is to get through the crisis. If you were forced to retire or separate due to medical conditions, mandatory retirement, being passed over for promotion, downsizing/retention issues, or disciplinary actions, the more impacting the crisis will be. Fairly logical, right? Well, many studies have been done on this, and there are psychologists across the spectrum of opinions about it. We will talk about of few of them in this chapter.

An identity crisis impacts how you see yourself and will also force you to ask yourself about your purpose in life. The two are pretty much joined at the hip. We each find our service as more than an identity but also our purpose for living. Psychologist Erik Erikson believes that the identity is the most important aspect of a person's life. If you do not know your role in life, then you feel in life that you do not know the real you. Erikson is the one accredited to coming up with the concept of an identity crisis. He states that your identity is a psychosocial phenomenon in that in that your identity is "an interaction between someone's sense of who he or she is as a person in society's recognition of that person as an individual."[23] He suggests that people will go through an identity crisis at various points throughout their lives:[24]

- Career transition—beginning or ending a career
- Relationships—getting married or divorced
- Having children
- Death of a loved one
- Experiencing traumatic events (which we identify separately)
- Learning about a life-changing medical condition

Some symptoms of someone going through an identity crisis include asking the following questions:

- Who am I?
- What is my purpose and/or role in society?
- What kind of work am I going to do now?
- What is the real purpose of my life?
- Who do I want to spend my life with and where?
- What do I think spiritually, and what are my values?
- What am I passionate about, and what am I going to do now?
- What are my interests and hobbies?

---

[23] Gourguechon, Prudy. 2019. "The Second Identity Crisis: How to Deal in a Smart Way with a New Phase of Life." *Forbes*.

[24] Cherry, Kendra. 2019. "Identity Crisis: How Our Identity Forms out of Conflict."

For military and first responders (this applies to other professional occupations too), when they separate or retire from service, they "may grieve the loss of their professional identity." People who serve "thrive on the socialization, the busyness… [and the] sense of mission."[25] An identity crisis and lack of defined purpose can turn into wounds (psychological/emotional but also social), especially among men, who derive much of their self-worth from their occupation. Women typically establish their self-worth on more than just their occupation because they assimilate more with relationships.[26] But both will suffer from this crisis.

As a chaplain or minister, helping someone in transition from their service will be a regular occurrence. A good technique is to ask them these questions and get them to think about each answer. Do not answer the questions for them. They own their own answers, and it is important to help talk them through their answers so they can reshape their identity and define their purpose for themselves. You are the facilitator of that discussion. They may not have all the answers right away. Some people will just need time for "soul searching" or introspection for those answers. This is where you need to remain in contact with them and continue to help them get to these answers.

The following are ways to help combat isolation and help someone redefine their purpose:

- Pursue a longtime hobby or try a new hobby desire; join a club
- Volunteer in the community/give back
- Pursue an occupational passion to serve driven by passion, not a paycheck
- Teach or mentor those in the previous occupation
- Return to school
- Start a new career
- Coach/participate in sports

---

25 Stettner, Morey. 2018. "Adrift and Alone in Retirement? Rebuild Your Identity, Therapists Say." MarketWatch.

26 Ibid.

Your job as a chaplain or minister is not only to assist them to find out what they are going to do but also to remind them of who they are in Christ. Some may struggle so much that they need more professional help. I strongly recommend a Christian counselor, not a psychologist. There are significant issues with psychology because they all take a secular view to defining who they are when this is a time to get in touch with what God says they are and what God wants them to do with their lives.

Issues with Secular Psychology

"...every good tree bears good fruit, but a bad tree bears bad fruit. A good tree cannot bear bad fruit, and a bad tree cannot bear good fruit" (Matthew 7:17–18).

The primary issue I see with secular (not Christian based) psychology is that it lacks God in the session. For the average Christian, we know we have identity and purpose in Christ, even if we cannot fully define it. Sometimes we turn to psychologists for help. But psychologists will not give you a godly answer. That is the reason why.

It is extremely important to choose a Christian counselor over a psychologist!

Some Christian counselors are licensed psychologists and call themselves Christian psychologists. However, the terms *Christian* and *psychology* are conflicted. That is why I choose to refer to them as Christian counselors because they use the Bible, and they use the example of Christ as being the great counselor.

"For unto us a child is born, unto us a Son is given; and the government will be upon his shoulder. And his name will be called wonderful, counselor, mighty God, everlasting Father, Prince of Peace" (Isaiah 9:6 NIV).

Psychology is far from biblical and far from what Jesus teaches about counseling. Yet this is often where people go when they suffer from an identity crisis. We even have churches, community leaders, ministry leaders, and family members referring those who serve(d) to psychologists or psychiatrists (a medical practitioner specializing in the diagnosis and treatment of mental illness). Therefore, it is imperative we take a moment and go over psychology.

Common psychology camps/disciplines. Humanism (*Oxford* definition)—"an outlook or system of thought attaching prime importance to human rather than divine or supernatural matters." Humanist beliefs stress the potential value and goodness of human beings, emphasize common human needs, and seek solely rational ways of solving human problems.

Humanism started with Friedrich Niethammer and referred to "a perspective that affirms some notion of human freedom and progress. It views humans as solely responsible for the promotion and development of individuals and emphasizes a concern for man in relation to the world."[27] This discipline essentially states that humans are responsible for everything that has occurred in the world and removes the notion that God has any role in it. It also describes people as being essentially good where the Bible teaches that people are inherently evil.

"But the things that come out of a person's mouth come from the heart, and these defile them. For out of the heart come evil thoughts—murder, adultery, sexual immorality, theft, false testimony, slander" (Matthew 15:18-19 NIV).

Behaviorism (*Oxford* definition)—"the theory that human and animal behavior can be explained in terms of conditioning, without appeal to thoughts or feelings, and that psychological disorders are best treated by altering behavior patterns."

Several people formed what is known as behaviorism. "Edward Thorndike pioneered the law of effect, a procedure that involved the use of consequences to strengthen or weaken behavior. Edward Thorndike worked on comparative psychology and this lead to the Theory of Connectionism. With these findings Edward Thorndike

[27] Domenic Marbaniang. 2009. "Developing the Spirit of Patriotism and Humanism in Children for Peace and Harmony," *Children At Risk: Issues and Challenges*, Jesudason Jeyaraj (ed.), Bangalore: CFCD/ISPCK: p. 474.

was able to establish the foundation for educational psychology."[28] So the basis of all psychology that is taught is based on the idea that human behavior, as well as animal behavior, can be explained as either normal or a disorder and can be treated with behavior modification. However, we know the difference between right and wrong, and we know as Christians what is righteous and sinful. We are accountable for sin biblically and that Jesus died for our sins if we are in Him. But sin comes at a cost.

Psychoanalytic (*Oxford* definition)—"a system of psychological theory and therapy which aims to treat mental disorders by investigating the interaction of conscious and unconscious elements in the mind and bringing repressed fears and conflicts into the conscious mind by techniques such as dream interpretation and free association."

This psychoanalytic approach/discipline "was established in the early 1890s by Austrian neurologist Sigmund Freud, who retained the term psychoanalysis for his own school of thought."[29] It is amazing that the Greek work for *psycho* is soul when the church is the one who traditionally deals with matters of the soul, and this analysis has nothing to do with the soul. It appears more appropriate to say it is analysis of the mind. Even then, there is little analytics involved. A typical session includes uncovering your feelings about an issue and guiding you to accepting how that impacts your life.

Psychodynamic (*Oxford* definition)—"the interrelation of the unconscious and conscious mental and emotional forces that determine personality and motivation."

This discipline was based on Freud's psychoanalysis but refined by several of his followers, Carl Jung, Alfred Adler, and Melanie Klein. It is essentially a discipline that explains why people do what they do. "At the heart of psychological processes, according to Freud, is the ego, which he envisions as battling with three forces: the id, the

---

[28] "Life and Work of Edward Lee Thorndike Philosophy Essay," UKEssays.com. Retrieved 2020-05-04.

[29] Mitchell, Juliet. 2000. *Psychoanalysis and Feminism: A Radical Reassessment of Freudian Psychoanalysis*. London: Penguin Books: p. 341.

superego, and the outside world."[30] In modern application, therapy sessions are more focused on identifying areas of life conflicts and working through conflict resolution.

Important ministry note: Freud was not a Christian; he was an atheist.

Although Sigmund Freud was of Jewish heritage and raised on Judaism beliefs, Freud was very skeptical and later rejected religion. Patrick Glynn stated in his review that "Freud believed the credibility of religion must be destroyed. It was, quite simply, the 'enemy'... In [his book] *The Future of an Illusion* (1927) he branded faith as a form of mental disorder, a 'universal obsessional neurosis,' rooted in 'infantile' and 'narcissistic' patterns of thought."

Darwinism has also made its way into psychology. Dr. Robert Watson said, "Darwin...kept a diary of his infant son... This record was one of the sources for the beginning of modern child psychology." Dr. Robert Woodworth stated, "Another very important influence came from Darwin and the theory of evolution. For if all animals are blood relatives in respect to bodily structure must they not be the same in respect to behavior and mentality?" Dr. Carl Jung explained, "Of course, to win for one's self a place in society and so transform one's nature that it is more or less fitted to this existence, is in every instance an important achievement."[31]

Dr. Tanya Dineen, a psychologist, left the psychology field after seeing what she claimed were "abuses" in the industry. She claims, "The Psychology Industry is separating people from their families, promoting stereotypic and hostile views of men and women, degrading friendship and generally promoting distrust and suspicion."[32] She also acknowledged that women far outnumber men as psychologists who often promoted woman taking headship over the family rather than men as the Bible states. Dineen added, "What is now called

---

[30] Freud, Sigmund. 1923. *The Ego and the Id.* W. W. Norton & Company: pp. 4–5. ISBN 0-393-00142-3.

[31] Shultz, Duane. 1981. *A History of Modern Psychology*, 3rd ed. Academic Press Inc.

[32] Dr. Tana Dineen. 1996. *Manufacturing Victims, What the Psychology Industry is Doing to People* Montreal: Robertt Davis Publishing: p. 98.

'psychology' is…'junk science'…with no soul or science, no boundaries and no method; swept along by the shifting ground of popular belief and ephemeral demands for expert opinion."[33]

This is the truth of psychology! All these disciplines are man-made and are void of the Holy Spirit. Psychology theories and techniques are predominately human solutions to spiritual issues. It most cases, this involves self-actualization, self-maintenance, and self-improvement. Although it can sound good, "such wisdom does not come from above but is earthly, unspiritual, demonic" (James 3:15 NIV).

Here is God's position:

For My thoughts are not your thoughts,
Neither are your ways My ways," declares the Lord.
"For as the heavens are higher than the earth,
So are My ways higher than your ways,
And My thoughts than your thoughts. (Isaiah 55:8 NIV)

Here are some striking differences between psychology and Christianity:

Man= Individual Man or Woman	Christianity	Psychology
Origin of Man	Creation (Genesis 1:26-27)	Evolution (Darwin)
Composition of Man	Body, Soul, and Spirit (1 Thessalonians 5:23)	Body and Soul (Psyche)
Nature of Man	Sinful (Romans 3:23)	Good
Responsibility of Man	Absolute (Galatians 5:19-21)	Relative
Control of Man	Conviction (1 John 1:8-9) Repentance (Matthew 4:17)	By self, by concious, or by behavior modification
Destiny of Man	Heaven (John 14:2-3) or Hell (Revelation 21:8)	None or Uncertain
Identity of Man	God's Image (Genesis 1:27) Child of God (John 1:12)	Self, society, achievements, family, titles
Pupose of Man	Labor in the Lord (1 Cor 15:58) Make Disciples (Matt 28-19-20)	Success, happiness, life enrichment

[33] Ibid., 138.

We could devote books to this topic, and many have. But I think we covered enough to make the point. If you need to refer someone to counseling, ensure it is a Christian counselor, biblical counselor, Christian psychologist, Christian psychiatrist, or if it is not evident in the name, ensure they are Christian and provide Christian principles in their counseling.

"Guard what has been entrusted to your care. Turn away from godless chatter and the opposing ideas of what is falsely called knowledge, which some have professed and in so doing have wandered from the faith. Grace be with you" (1 Timothy 6:20–21 NIV).

Identity Crisis Impact

The primary impact of an identity crisis is stress. Stress builds anxiety. Anxiety increases when faced with situations where we are unsure of the outcome, and the anxiety decreases when we start to realize that we have more control of a situation. It really is a survival instinct.

Military transition programs primarily focus on benefits and finding a new job. It does provide information about the Veterans Administration and Tricare for physical wounds, and the state's psychological services are there if you want them. There is no information presented on the challenges of cultural changes, relationship issues (social wounds), and spiritual wounds that can arrive from an identity crisis.

Because anxiety is such an intense self-preservation and uncertain emotion that a service member will go through, they often make poor transition decisions based on perceived desperation. Often, "veterans grab the first job or relationship that presents itself," which may lead to further issues. The job may be a "terrible fit" even though it may seem as a "safe bet" to at least have a job. But that is short-lived and can only compound, prolong, and complicate the issues of an identity crisis. For veterans who are single or divorced, entering a new relationship during transition often occurs as the person looks for stability and establishment in their identity. But having the "wrong relationship partner can create endless chaos in one's life."[34] It is common for veterans to jump into the first relationship just like they are prone to grab the first job presented to them. If either is not the right fit, they can feel trapped and frustrated. Too many veterans settle after their military careers. They have so much to offer society but do not plan prior to transition. Prior planning prevents poor decisions during transition.

Military leadership is often wasted when transitioning from service. Many have the potential to step into greater leadership roles in the civilian sector, but many veterans settle during a time of an identity crisis. To effectively transition, the service member needs to define their personal identity by determining their "values, purpose, intrinsic strengths, intentions, belief structure, and common factors for success—across an integrative program of transition that addresses the wellness, socialization, culture, and relational aspects of reintegration"[35] Military leaders spend a career shaping their leadership style and learning from their mistakes. If they can only focus on who they are, they can spend mental capital on what they will do next. Military leaders can discover the greatest opportunity to continue serving in society. Our society needs strong leaders, and they want to be inspired. Those who served in the military always wanted the world to be a better place and possess the skills to contribute in a leadership capacity.[36]

In a Military Family Lifestyle Survey conducted in 2018, over 47 percent of veterans reported that their transition experience was

---

[34] Springer, Shauna, PhD, and Roncoroni, Jason. 2019. "How the Stress of Military Transition leads to Regrettable Career and Relationship Decisions." *Military Times.*

[35] Ibid.

[36] Roncoroni, Jason, and Springer, Shauna, PhD. 2019. *Beyond the Military: A Leader's Handbook to Warrior Integration.* Available on Amazon.

"difficult" or "very difficult."[37] The survey provided the following results where a veteran responded to transition challenges:

- 45 percent of veterans felt a loss of connection to the military community.
- 82 percent felt the general public does not understand what military families face.
- 60 percent felt the public does not understand the value veterans bring to the community
- 39 percent reported a loss of camaraderie
- 47 percent reported not having a sense of purpose
- 64 percent felt they needed time to figure out what to do with their lives

The veterans of the survey also identified some areas that help. Having a strong support network, landing a job right away, and including spouses in the transition program significantly improve the transition period.[38]

Police departments and other first responder organizations typically do not have transition services. For police officers, retirement or separation from service causes stress, anxiety, and social challenges. Police officers develop strong bonds with other officers. They specifically see themselves as distinctly separate from society. When they leave service, they lose their status, their authority, their identity, and their sense of purpose. They lose much of their support network and will quickly miss sharing experiences, dangerous situations, being "in the know" of what is happening in the community, the bonds among officers, and the prestige of wearing the uniform. Many police officers have few transferable skills to other occupations that will land them a job, especially with the same level of prestige and excitement.[39]

---

[37] Blue Star Families. 2019. "The True Story of Our Veterans: Challenges of the Military Transition to Civilian Life."

[38] Ibid.

[39] Brandl, Stephen G. and Smith, Brad W. 2013. "An Empirical Examination of Retired Police Officers' Length of Retirement and Age at Death: A Research Note." *Police Quarterly* (March).

Identity in Christ

For those of you who are in ministry or have been a Christian for some time, you know that your identity is in Christ. For some reason, this is simply not enough for veterans and first responders when they transition. Having retired after twenty-seven years in the Army, I would like to believe it was enough for me. But I was praying like mad for something more. For me, it mostly had to do with the "what was next" or my purpose after the Army, not my identity. I knew that I was a child of God. I knew that I was His. I just had to strip the labels of my rank, put away the uniforms, and get used to not being saluted. I mentioned previously a couple of the tricks that worked for me. I showed contractor identification when getting on base to prevent from being saluted. I had to stop telling people I just retired from the Army. I have had friends who grew out a beard or let their hair grow long. My wife did not like the beard I tried to grow, and I was losing my hair too much to let it grow. However, the most important realization is that your identity is not in what you do but who you are in Christ. It is that obvious to us, but if someone's faith is not that strong or they have no faith at all, they can have a crisis on their hand.

I mentioned before that every veteran and first responder will go through an identity crisis, even the strongest of Christians. This has to do more with how people see you than you see yourself. I am a contractor now, but I do not like being referred to as a contractor. I am a volunteer chaplain, but volunteer work is not seen by society as an identity item. Next thing I know, I am telling them I recently retired from the Army, which is another aspect I was trying to get away from. Don't get me wrong. I am proud of my serving our country and am grateful I have a contracting job. I enjoy being a volunteer chaplain of the Niceville Police Department, and I enjoy telling people about our ministry. But none of these things are who I am.

So I end up using family as part of that identification, which is also acceptable in society. I am married, and I have three girls and a dog. So society knows I have a family. We do not identify ourselves as a Christian in society. But being a child of God is the most important identifying component of me. However, who goes about and says, "Hello, my name is Michael Belton, and I am a Christian." That sums up a large part of me, but I do not go around saying that, and I guess neither do you. I also do not think it will change in American society when Christianity is so offensive to so many people. I will defend the fact that I am a Christian, but I do not throw it out there when I meet someone.

For ministry, it is important to help the veteran or the first responder acknowledge their identity in Christ. Then you can work with them on their purpose. For those who do not know Christ, I ask them to describe how they see themselves. They will inevitably tell me about what they do and how change is making them feel a little lost. My suggestion, do not use this as an opportunity to get on an evangelical campaign and feel like you need to share the "good news" right there. Remember, veterans and first responders do not make sound decisions in time of transition. Instead, share how you identify yourself through Christ. Allow the Holy Spirit to work in their lives. If you are working with them, they should see Christ in you, and the opportunity will present itself in His timing to lead that person to Christ.

Christian author Jerry Bridges answers this question, Who am I? And our identity in Christ. He used the scripture to unlock eight answers: I am a new creature, I am in Christ, I am justified, I am an adopted son of God, I am a new creation, I am a saint, I am a servant of Jesus Christ, and I am not yet perfect.[40]

Christian author Luke Finley answers the Who am I? question this way. He states that people try to define their identity in three areas—"what you do, what people think of you, and what you have." He further states that you will not find "lasting peace" if this is what you value as your identity. He mentioned Nouwen, who warns that "death will eliminate each identity: you won't be able to accomplish more, people will forget about you, and you will lose all of your possessions." The answer as he puts it is, "I am God's beloved." Because he identifies with Christ, he is no longer concerned about working so

[40] Bridges, Jerry. 2012. *Who Am I? Identity in Christ.*

hard to achieve the most, make everyone like him, and to get more stuff.[41]

Look at the life of Jesus when he was here on earth. How did he enter the earth, and how did he live while he was here? In society standards, most would have considered him to be a failure. He was a blue-collar worker, a carpenter who left carpentry to go into ministry. His ministry lasted only three years before perceptively falling apart and being ridiculed and rejected of his claims. He was accused, tried, and sentenced to death at a young age. He never had any earthly possessions, no established earthy title or position, did not live in a great home, did not accumulate wealth and great stuff, or even seen as associating with the right people.[42] We know the reality of it all. Jesus knew His identity in the Father, and He knew his purpose.

Purpose in Christ

"But you are a chosen people, a royal priesthood, a holy nation, God's special possession, that you may declare the praises of him who called you out of darkness into his wonderful light" (1 Peter 2:9 NIV).

When I talk to people about their purpose in life for God, I am often amazed how many people get defensive and try to change the narrative. Sometimes I will even get more assertive and ask, What are you doing for the kingdom, and want is God wanting you to do? I have my fellow brothers and sisters in Christ then attempt to tell me that they do not have to do anything (which is true) and that their salvation is not based on works (also true). But who was talking about salvation? To frame this correctly, I often tell people they have two primary purposes to life:

1. To "make a decision" to either accept or deny Christ, no decision and Satan gets you by default.
2. What is God's purpose for your life?

---

[41] Finley, Luke. 2019. "How Do You Answer the Question: 'Who am I?'" https://www.lukefinley.com.

[42] Ibid.

Many theologians even talk about God's plan but will often fall short of acknowledging that each person who comes to know Christ is selected and has a divine purpose. Here are a few verses to reflect on:

> "For I know the plans I have for you," declares the LORD, "plans to prosper you and not to harm you, plans to give you hope and a future." (Jeremiah 29:11 NIV)

> "Many are the plans in a person's heart, but it is the LORD's purpose that prevails." (Proverbs 19:21 NIV)

> "And we know that in all things God works for the good of those who love him, who have been called according to his purpose." (Romans 8:28 NIV)

> "For we are God's handiwork, created in Christ Jesus to do good works, which God prepared in advance for us to do." (Ephesians 2:10 NIV)

> "May God himself, the God of peace, sanctify you through and through. May your whole spirit, soul and body be kept blameless at the coming of our Lord Jesus Christ." (1 Thessalonians 5:23 NIV)

> "Therefore, my dear brothers and sisters, stand firm. Let nothing move you. Always give yourselves fully to the work of the Lord, because you know that your labor in the Lord is not in vain." (1 Corinthians 15:58 NIV)

> "Therefore, go and make disciples of all nations, baptizing them in the name of the Father and of the Son and of the Holy Spirit, and teaching

> them to obey everything I have commanded you. And surely, I am with you always, to the very end of the age." (Matthew 28:19–20 NIV)

The above seven verses tell you all you need to know about your purpose. I often say, if the only thing you had to do in this life was to accept Christ, then the Lord would take you at that moment. You are still here for a reason. I also say, if you had the opportunity to get a short visit or get to see heaven, then you would not want to be here. Most of us would probably be offended by having to stay here. The only reason you are still here is because you have a purpose to be here...a God-given purpose.

"The most important thing in life is not what you do, but who you become" (Dallas Willard).

Mainstream society (or culture) has it all wrong. Man trying to search for the meaning and the purpose of life is a multibillion-dollar industry. People write books, make movies, and become life coaches, motivational speakers, life strategists, psychologists, and more trying to convince people that their purpose in life is the "emergence of what you would like to experience." They will tell you that asking who you are is the wrong questions to ask and that we should ask ourselves, "How would I like to experience my life?"[43] Dr. Scott Allison, professor of psychology at the University of Richmond, suggests our purpose is not what other people claim: to find happiness, love others, become a better version of you, follow God's will, or even have no purpose at all. He suggests our purpose is "to live the life of a hero."[44]

Life coach Simon T. Bailey said the movie *The Lion King* changed his life when Mufasa said, "Simba! Remember who you are. You are more than what you have become." He has since spoken to over 1,600 organizations in forty-five countries, coached over one

---

[43] Schwartz, Mel. 2010. "Who Am I? A Far Better Question to Ask Yourself, 'How Would I Like to Experience My Life?' *Psychology Today*.

[44] Allison, Scott T. 2014. "What Is Your Purpose in Life? Here Are Four Truths That Give Your Life Meaning and Purpose."

hundred company leaders, and has written nine books. He believes and coaches that your "purpose" is to be curious, know your motives, spark you intuition, evaluate your life (even suggest soul-searching), develop impactful habits, and do what makes you excited to get out of bed every morning.[45] In essence, he defines your purpose at achieving success and achieving to be significant. In his view, your purpose is to live your dreams. No wonder he has achieved so much success. He is inspiring others who want to be successful too, who think this is their real purpose in life.

In my lifetime, I have seen so many "great people" do some incredible things. Most men love sports and become fans of athletes who achieve greatness. We have seen so many of them. In basketball, Michael Jordan comes to mind. In baseball, for me, it was Cal Ripken Jr. In football, it is Tom Brady. In golf, it is Tiger Woods. In hockey, it is Wayne Gretzky…and the list goes on. Each of us has our favorites. I am a huge Washington Redskins fan, and my favorite player of all time is Hall of Famer no. 28 Cornerback Darrell Green. Most view these men as having a God-given talent. But this extends to other industries. How about names like Bill Gates (Microsoft) and Steve Jobs (Apple)? How about famous singers like Michael Jackson, Cher, Madonna, Whitney Houston, and Mariah Carey? What about movie stars like Harrison Ford, Tom Hanks, Julia Roberts, and Kevin Costner? All these names can be argued as having a God-given gift. Or do they? Is it something we just say, or is it true? I do not know if any or all these people know Christ or not. I do not know any of these people, nor have I met them. A point to remember is this: if it is truly a God-given gift and that is their real purpose, then would there not be a kingdom focus to it and one where God is honored?

Then there are others like Joseph Carter who believe "the universe doesn't care about your purpose." He points to Aristotle, who believes the universe was "saturated" with purpose. That Aristotle, in his Nicomachean ethics, believes our purpose is happiness and eudaemonia "well-spiritedness" and that everyone strives for happiness. However, Carter rejects Aristotle because he believes it is not

[45] Bailey, Simon T. 2018. "What Is My Purpose in Life?" Success at www.success.com.

about happiness. He is a materialist and claims the universe operates without purpose. He claims there is no purpose to life and that you and I are "enormously insignificant." He states everything to the contrary is simply a myth or a story. Cosmologist and theoretical physicist Sean Carroll believes purpose "aren't built into the architecture of the universe, they emerge as ways of talking about our human-scale environment." Anthropologist Dean Falk suggests as an evolutionist that we are goal oriented, and the purpose of human evolution is for us to believe in our species. German philosopher Hans Blumenberg suggested our purpose "springs from our longing for permanence." Carter believes that love, forgiveness, and friendships are for our benefit and that war, oppression, and conflict are self-inflicted, and we do not need to look at God but ourselves.[46]

In ministry, we will be faced with people who simply will reject God. Evolutionists are primarily atheists. Lawrence Krauss assertively stated, "The fact that we evolved on this planet is just a 'cosmic accident', and people who believe otherwise are probably suffering from some kind of religious delusion."[47] People like this simply detract from the truth about God. They impact everyday society and therefore even confuse the most devout of Christians into believing that our purpose is something more or something less than that of God's purpose for our life.

This is where I come back to our main verse for our ministry: "Therefore, my dear brothers and sisters, stand firm. Let nothing move you. Always give yourselves fully to the work of the Lord, because you know that your labor in the Lord is not in vain" (1 Corinthians 15:58 NIV).

We must remember whose side we are on. We are on God's side! We must remain firm in our faith, read our Bibles, pray earnestly, and labor in the Lord. Our purpose is His purpose. We can read about all the blessings and rewards in the Bible. But we can be assured that a purpose without God is no purpose at all.

---

[46] Carter, Joseph P. 2017. "The Universe Doesn't Care About Your 'Purpose'" *The New York Times.*

[47] Krauss, Lawrence. 2017. *The Greatest Story Ever Told...So Far.*

Review Questions

1. Why is transitioning from being in the military or being a first responder so impactful on our identity that it leads to an identity crisis?
2. What are some of the ways to mitigate the impact of an identity crisis?
3. What are some of the issues with secular psychology?
4. When someone is suffering from an identity crisis and you are looking to refer them to counseling, what should you be looking for and why?
5. Explain your identity in Christ.
6. Explain your purpose in Christ.
7. What do you think the biggest challenges will be in ministering when encountered with people who do not take a God-focused approach to identity and purpose?

CHAPTER 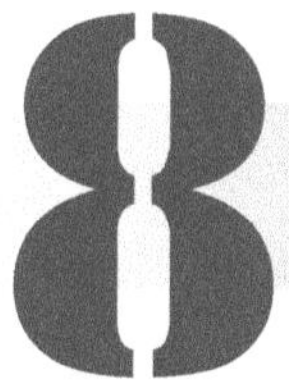

GOD-GIVEN PURPOSE

Then I heard the voice of the Lord, saying, "Whom shall I send, and who will go for Us?" Then I said, "Here am I. Send me!

—Isaiah 6:8 NIV

Determining what God's purpose is for our life is a challenging quest. I see so many Christians struggle with finding their purpose in life. While some do not feel God has a purpose for them, others feel that once you are saved, God really is not expecting anything out of them other than to live a Christian life. However, many know they should serve in some capacity but wish the "calling" from God was more direct...like an angel of the Lord appearing to them and just telling them what to do. For His reason, He puts us on a journey to seek Him, and He reveals our purpose in His timing. It can be frustrating to figure out, but that is His way. I find that even those who are assured that they know what their calling is end up running from it like Jonah.

The truth is, we all have a purpose. Otherwise, we would not still be here. Unfortunately, most Christians will go through life and never answer God's call. What a horrible thought. You spend your whole life living doing what you want, and you never do what God had planned for you. You never get the blessings, the rewards, and never experience life to the fullest because you lived your life your way and not His way. You miss out on a truly connected and deep relationship with Christ. But that is the beauty or perhaps the issue with complete free will. We can choose to accept God or deny Him. We can choose to serve Him or choose not to. We can choose our way or His way. He will not force us to step up to the call, so unfortunately, most do not.

> As a prisoner for the Lord, then, I urge you to live a life worthy of the calling you have received. Be completely humble and gentle; be patient, bearing with one another in love. Make every effort to keep the unity of the Spirit through the bond of peace. There is one body and one Spirit, just as you were called to one hope when you were called; one Lord, one faith, one baptism; one God and Father of all, who is over all and through all and in all. (Ephesians 4:1–6 NIV)

We all have a story. Some of the greatest people I know in ministry have amazing stories. They all endured significant challenges, and they all admit they are still on the journey. I do not like sharing my story, but I will here because it makes an important point. Serving God will be the greatest challenge of your life. As the verse says, you will be a prisoner for the Lord. I think there is reason for it: for humility, for transformation, for understanding, for strength, for wisdom, and for preparedness. Some want it to be easy and look for God to "part the Red Sea" and clear the path where we are not touched by a drop of water. But it is not going to happen, and the path to your purpose will come with significant hardship. I will declare that it must be this way. God is transforming you from what you want to be to what He wants you to be.

For me, I did not come up in a Christian household and did not come to know Christ until I was twenty-one. I told this story briefly in chapter 1. What I failed to mention then is that I was on a roller coaster for the next seventeen years in my walk with Christ. I went through seasons from going to church and feeling connected to a season of rebellion and placing my faith on the back burner. It is an all too common story of how most Christians live. We have periods where our faith is hot and when it is cold. The problem is, as long as you are saved and as long as you try to live a good life, be faithful to your family, do well at work, and treat others well, then you generally think you are doing what God wants you to do. I have found that this is not always the case, and sometimes, God must really get your attention.

In 2008, I had my "divine intervention" from the Lord on a TDY trip in Virginia. Something came over me. I could not eat, could not sleep, and was pulled to the scripture. Next thing I knew, I was frantically taking notes and praying around the clock. The result, I felt the Lord calling me to seminary. The problem was the timing was horrible. I was in the Army, and I was three-fourths the way through a PhD program in sports management with a 4.0 GPA. My dream was to get into football and perhaps be a coach or general manager of a professional team. I also moonlighted as a high school coach the six previous years. But the calling was so indescribably intense that I started researching seminary schools. I had no way to pay for it, knew nothing about it, had no idea if my wife would support the idea, nor what I was going to do after completing it. I had so much time and money invested in my PhD program. But I absolutely knew that the path I wanted was not God's path. I cannot explain how; I just knew. The time in prayer was an intense connection, and I knew God was calling me to seminary for some unknown reason. I had no idea if God wanted me to be a pastor, a military chaplain, or a missionary. He did not reveal that to me then. He revealed that I needed to just go to seminary.

I left that TDY trip and went home and told my wife that I was called by God to go to seminary. She was shocked, speculative, and I got that look from her that any guy would get from their wife. That nonverbal look of, "Really?" She even told me, "Coaching is your dream. I thought that is what you wanted to do when you got out of the Army?" What she was saying was all true. But I went on to tell her I was dropping out of my PhD program immediately, giving up on coaching football, and would be applying for seminary. I do not think she believed me until I did those things. All signs pointed to Liberty University. I applied, was accepted, and was approved for college loans. I no longer pursued football, and I officially dropped out of my PhD program, which even caught the school by surprise. Everything changed from that point.

From talking to so many people, they do not get that moment that they are sure God is talking directly to them. But I did. I am not going to profess to know why. What I will profess is that the more you seek Him, the more He reveals, and we will go over later in the chapter how to get connected with your purpose. I want to share with you a few truths to either help you find that purpose that God has for you specifically or help you gain focus and determination to do what he has already called you to do. Oswald Chambers said, "As Christians we are not here for our own purpose at all—we are here for the purpose of God, and the two are not the same." I felt my purpose was to retire someday from the Army and coach football. It was God's purpose for me to forcibly retired from the Army and go into ministry. This was His plan that I would love to tell you was one that I was completely obedient to, but I was not.

"'For I know the plans I have for you,' declares the Lord, 'plans to prosper you, and not to harm you, plans to give you hope and a future'" (Jeremiah 29:11 NIV).

I started attending seminary at night, and that journey would take me the next six years. I struggled because I did not know the Bible very well. I had no idea that it would be so hard. I struggled writing papers, struggled with professors, the tests, and my own competitive ego. I struggled having to learn Greek and Hebrew. I went from having a 4.0 GPA in a sports management PhD program to having about a 3.4 GPA in a master of divinity program, and I felt like I was working 10× harder at it. The reading was exhausting, and I found myself doubting whether I made the right decision. Then I realized that my decision was just to be obedient. This was God's plan for me. But that plan came with many storms.

I was struggling to find balance between an Army career, family, and attending seminary. I used my leave time to take courses at the main campus. Fortunately, we could take all classes online. However, I also wanted to experience what seminary campus life was like. It was amazing but short-lived. But the storms kept on coming; the struggles were real. It was no fun, all work, and all school all the time. I questioned myself, my calling, what I was doing, and whether I could keep going. I remember pleading with God that everything was too challenging, and to soften the burden, I prayed for wisdom, for strength, and for stronger faith. I did not feel that I was getting any of it. We were living in Maryland, and the storms got worse. My wife and I started having marriage issues. She almost left me, and instead, I found myself living on the couch of my friend Raymond Shindledecker for a month. My life was a complete mess, and I was still taking seminary classes, worrying about the next test or paper I needed to write. Right about the time my wife and I semiworked through our issues, I was transferred to Germany to be part of Special Operations Command-Europe (SOCEUR).

I got to SOCEUR, and we struggled with living on the German economy. I am struggling with simple things like getting a solid internet connection to get my classwork done, getting my family settled in a new home, working through how to get utilities in Germany, etc. To make matters worse, a couple of months later, I was faced with a deployment to Afghanistan. I was stressed out, my family was stressed, my job was not going too well, I was struggling to keep up with classwork, and I was faced with a deployment. My wife was fed up with living on the Germany economy, so I used my deployment status to get my command to sponsor moving my family on-post. We moved again and then then immediately deployed, with many boxes still packed for my wife to deal with. The deployment had its highs and lows. I went as an effects officer, ultimately did threat finance human intelligence work, and developed a process to get Afghan National-level warrants from the Ministry of Interior for Counterintelligence. Ironically, I was assigned to a chaplain's position (which I think was a hint from God), which I ignored, and did human intelligence (HUMINT) instead. We would get warrants and have special forces teams mentor Afghan teams to conduct the arrests. I was able to pull off the greatest capture and detainment of a Taliban member that defined that deployment, but with constant friction with leadership to make it happen, I did not get the recognition for it. Looking back on it, I did not serve anyone on that deployment. I was trying to make a name for myself. I certainly was not a chaplain, but I was not even a good person. I can blame it on war, but in a way, I was in my element, thirsty for adventure. It was my war; it was not His. I was even extended over in Afghanistan that doubled my length of tour with no warning. But in a way, I was okay with it.

When I returned from Afghanistan, I found out I was disenrolled from the seminary because I missed a semester, and the Liberty University policy was to remain actively enrolled for the entire seminary program. My deployment broke that. I continued to struggle at work and at home. The homecoming honeymoon was short-lived before I had problems at the home front again, and I was out of the seminary program. My wife hated Germany, and I curtained out of there after much drama and went to Human Resources Command at Fort Knox in Kentucky. I got back into church and praying, started leading men's groups, led Bible study groups, and was able to get a letter of recommendation from my pastor for reinstatement into seminary. I presented my case to the administration office, provided proof of my deployment, and presented my letter of recommendation. I waited for weeks for a board to convene before being accepted back into seminary. I remember praying to God, "Why is this path so difficult? What am I going wrong?" But I made up my mind. "Until I get an answer from you, God, I am going to complete what You had me start."

"Trust in the Lord with all your heart and lean not on your own understanding; In all your ways acknowledge Him, and He shall direct your paths" (Proverbs 3:5–6).

I graduated seminary in 2014 with two master's degrees, one in religion and the other in divinity. I was so burned out from school emotionally and mentally. It was so bad that I would not focus anytime I tried to read something. I would have to read emails or notes multiple times because my brain simply could not process what I was reading. Work got hectic, my deputy at HRC died, and I went through the hiring process of getting a new deputy. I ended up having medical issues and even had colon surgery. And then before I knew it, we had a chance to take an assignment in Florida as a liaison for the Air Force at Hurlburt Field. We moved, and my dream was to be a colonel or even a general in the Army. I felt my chances were rather good too. So "my plan/my dream" was to continue with my career for as long as it would take me. Then another major storm occurred. I started having more major internal organ medical issues. I was hospitalized, and my lab work came back with abnormal readings. So another major storm, and I was like, "Really?" I went on a TDY trip to Germany and ended up in the hospital again. The doctor told me I had leukemia, and I needed treatment from an oncologist.

The weeks that followed were filled with fear and uncertainty as more tests were conducted when I got back home to Florida to find out the severity of my leukemia. My wife was scared that she would have to start preparing for life after me and raising our children on her own. I went to prayer and accepted that there was a real possibility that I was dying. I prepared my family the next several weeks. The more testing that occurred and the more secretive and cryptic the doctors were being with me, which gave me the sense that I would soon be appearing before Jesus. I reached a point where I accepted it. I felt I died to Christ before, and I was more worried about my family. I knew I could have died many times before and almost did on a couple of deployments both in Iraq and Afghanistan. But a peace came over me faced with death. I prayed again and asked why he put me through everything, and I got my answer.

You know your answer is from God when it is not your plan. Many times, I prayed for God to move mountains to make my plan happen, but He was making His plan happen. The leukemia results came back, and it was mostly positive with mixed reviews. On the one hand, I was stable and not dying, and I could potentially live with this condition for a long time. On the other hand, it is incurable, and any treatment will only be to keep it under control. But I did not need treatment for now. Then the next storm happened. I was referred against my will for a Medical Evaluation Board (MEB) in the Army. I was declared not only nondeployable but also unfit for active duty service both by the Army and the Veterans Administration. I was forced into retirement within ninety days of notification. I had no idea what I was going to do. All my plans and career aspirations ended instantly. Now I was worried about what I would do next. I went to prayer, and God put a strong sense on my heart to go into ministry. I remember saying, "Okay, God, I get it. You are taking the military away from me because I am supposed to be in ministry." But the storms did not stop. I figured I would become a pastor. I already knew many of the pastors in the area. I expressed my desire to be a pastor with each of them. I mentioned I was available for anyone who wanted to interview me, but no interviews came. I prayed, I was silent, I was still, I was doing everything the Bible was telling me to do, and…nothing! So I took the James 1:2–5 approach:

> Consider it pure joy, my brothers and sisters, whenever you face trials of many kinds, because you know that the testing of your faith produces perseverance. Let perseverance finish its work so that you may be mature and complete, not lacking anything. If any of you lacks wisdom, you should ask God, who gives generously to all without finding fault, and it will be given to you. (James 1:2–5 NIV)

I needed wisdom, I needed to understand, and I wanted answers of what God was doing with me. I need Him to answer what I was still living for. If I was going to remain alive at this point after wars, after major illnesses, after having the military taken away from me, after almost losing my family, and after not a single interview for ministry, I needed to understand my purpose. I was stuck. Then God took care of an immediate need like He always does. A contracting job surprisingly opened where I was working with my military unit I was retiring from. They wanted to hire me, and I was hired within a week. That provided security for my family. I praised God but still asked Him what His plan was for me.

Then an amazing thing happened. I started talking to veteran after veteran about their deployment issues, the struggles they were facing, and I started helping them. One of them said, "You should start a ministry to help us." So I tried to start a military ministry at my church. I will leave the church nameless, but they had a strategy to plant churches along what they called was the military highway to minister to the military. When I presented the possibility of having a military ministry, they told he, "That really is not within our culture." I was so perplexed and actually offended as a twenty-seven-year Army veteran that my church that I served and ministered in for over two years had a strategy to plant churches around military installations around the country without having a ministry to actually minister to them. So I just kept on praying and serving the Lord, one veteran at a time. Then I felt God tell me that I am doing what He wants. I need to use my experiences and my gifts to help my fellow veterans.

"As each one has received a gift, minister it to one another, as good stewards of the manifold grace of God" (1 Peter 4:10).

I needed to organize my efforts. Others impressed on me that this was a real ministry and meeting real needs in the community. After much prayer, I formed a strategic plan. I asked God to bless it if it was His will. He did, and that was the birth of Serve Ministries Inc. (SMI). But that did not end. I had mentors who said there were many police officers who could use help and other first responders as well. I was being introduced to people at a high rate. Need after need, first responders looking for hope. My mentor, Jack Crans, said, "You need to open up your ministry to first responders too." So I did. Then another amazing thing happened. I met a guy named Al Neidbalski who said I would be perfect for the Niceville Police Department chaplain position. I was hesitant because I was never a police officer. But he set up the meeting for me to meet the chief of police, David Popwell, and I became their chaplain immediately. Then I was being introduced to community leaders who said there were huge unmet needs concerning veterans and first responders in the community, so I took on the mission to help them one at a time. I realized I needed help to help more people. Many people wanted to help, but they did not know how. So that birthed out training and education program to make disciples. It all grew into a chaplaincy program, and we are still growing...following the needs of our veterans and first responders. I do not know how it will all go over time, but I trust that God does. It is His ministry; my purpose is to serve.

So another storm came when my wife went on a mission trip with that church (the same one that turned down the military ministry), and she had a huge falling out with the church's executive director and the pastor upon her return. I tried to calm things over unsuccessfully and then was experiencing marriage issues because my wife felt I was not defending her through it. So we left the church. A veteran and close friend I met through our daughters invited me to a church where he was one of the pastors on staff. He showed me they had a military ministry, so that was where we ended up going. But it was still rough. I almost went through a divorce. My wife was angry that I did not defend her like she expected and was angry at our church. She ended up not wanting to deal with either. I cried out to God and asked, "How am I supposed to minister to people in this community if my wife leaves me and I end up getting a divorce?" Miraculously, things changed. We only attended two marriage counseling sessions. But we patched things up. Ministry started thriving, and it's been going at one hundred miles per hour ever since.

What is my God-given purpose? Well, I think you know that now. I had to die to Christ to find it. I had to transform from who I was to what God wanted me to be. I had to live to a higher standard to represent God to the veterans, first responders, community leaders, church pastors, and other ministry leaders. I had to give up my will for His. I had to weather the storms and be transformed.

"Therefore, I urge you, brothers and sisters, in view of God's mercy, to offer your bodies as a living sacrifice, holy and pleasing to God—this is your true and proper worship. Do not conform to the pattern of this world but be transformed by the renewing of your mind. Then you will be able to test and approve what God's will is—his good, pleasing, and perfect will" (Romans 12:1–2 NIV).

Important for Your Ministry

You must ask God what you specifically are called to do. What is your God-given purpose? Pastor Rick Warren says it this way:

"Self-help books often suggest that you try to discover the meaning and purpose of your life by looking within yourself…but…that is the wrong place to start. You must begin with God, your Creator, and His reasons for creating you. You were made by God and for God, and until you understand that, life will never make sense." You can also get lost in your career and in everyday life thinking that is your purpose when, chances are, it is not. Rick Warren said, "I was lost seeking worldly things like money, power, women, and status but felt they were trivial because long term they don't matter. I knew we all must face death, so I decided to serve a purpose that's bigger than myself. We all want to leave a legacy, but I asked myself, how can I do that in a way that can truly makes an impact on others' lives?"[48] Rick Warren further explains our true purpose:

- We were made for God's pleasure.
- We were formed to be part of the family of God.
- We were created to be Christlike.
- We are shaped to serve God.
- We all have a mission.

People also are far too much into the notion of having an earthly legacy. All things related to earth are perishable. Your earthly legacy will be too. Chances are a few generations removed, and nobody will remember your name, not even your family tree. Your money will all be disbursed or spent, and your possessions will most likely end up in a bump. Yet we spend most of our life trying to chase our profession, more money, and more stuff focused even on doing it for our family and call all that our legacy. Our real legacy is not an earthly one but a heavenly one. This does not mean that you should not leave an inheritance for you children because it is the right thing to do.

> A good man leaves an inheritance to his children's children. (Proverbs 13:22 NIV)

[48] Warren, Rick. 2007. *The Purpose Driven Life: What on Earth Am I Here For?*

An inheritance is different from a legacy. But we must ask how to set up a legacy that matters and where we should store up our treasures. This is what Jesus says:

> Do not store up for yourselves treasures on earth, where moths and vermin destroy, and where thieves break in and steal. But store up for yourselves treasures in heaven, where moths and vermin do not destroy, and where thieves do not break in and steal. For where your treasure is, there your heart will be also. (Matthew 6:19–20 NIV)

This also does not mean you cannot have a successful career and be wealthy. There are many who have both and still serve God like Tony Dungy, Joe Gibbs, Dave Ramsey, Tom Hanks, Carrie Underwood, Mark Wahlberg, Reba McEntire, Denzel Washington, and Tim Tebow, to name a few examples. There are many in business, sports, and entertainment who have found wealth and career success but remained grounded in their faith in God. They remained humble, and their success did not replace God with money.

> No one can serve two masters. Either you will hate the one and love the other, or you will be devoted to the one and despise the other. You cannot serve both God and money. (Matthew 6:24 NIV)

It can be argued that their successful certainly has an earthy legacy, but it can also be argued that they have had tremendous impact on lives that have a more eternal heavenly legacy. Which one do you think will last longer?

When you are trying to define your purpose in life, you can certainly consider what is best for your family, what you are going to do next for a career, if you need more education, your financial plans, and where you want to live. But, the no. 1 question you need to ask is, What is my God-given purpose?

No Excuses

Serving your God-given purpose will not be convenient. But really, what is? Your career, family, responsibilities, obligations, bills, taxes, etc. all are not convenient most the time. They all take time and require you to sacrifice something. Even your hobbies and interests are not always convenient, but you pursue them and sometimes prioritize them because that is what you desire to do. Your God-given purpose is no different, but I will propose it will even be more challenging than all the rest combined. The main reason is you have a great deceiver (Satan) who would rather you spend your time on anything else than God's purpose. So you have the forces of evil working against you. When the going gets tough, typically, the excuses start flowing. Do you think you are any exception? Examine your life. Can you honestly say that you prioritize God's will over everything else in your life, and are you serving the way He wants you to? Here are some common excuses that we can expect to encounter in ministry:

- *I do not have time.* The issue is with prioritizing what is important in life; everyone is busy.
- *I do not know the Bible.* Take time to learn, but start now. You will never completely memorize the Bible or completely understand it. But you can get stronger the more you are in it.
- *I do not need to do works to be saved.* True, but as previously discussed in a previous chapter, we are not talking about salvation. We are talking about your purpose.
- *I do not know what God wants of me.* He wants you to use your talents, your experiences, your passions to reach and help people. He wants you to lead them to Him and for you to invest in them to become disciples.
- *What if I am rejected?* They are not rejecting you; they are rejecting Christ.
- *What if I lose my friends?* Then they really are not your friends, and you will lose them eventually anyways because they will not end up where you are going. Plus, what kind

of friend does that make you if you do not want them to go to heaven?

- *I will lose my family*. Perhaps your earthly one but never your heavenly one. If you love your family, you will at least try.
- *I do not know what to say*. Speak from your heart, be real with people, do not profess to know everything, and be willing to study/learn together.
- *And the many things that run through your head that start with...what if?*

Answer: *Stop making excuses!*

Think of it this way. If you stood before Jesus, would you give Him all your excuses? I bet not. You would probably come clean and say that you simply did not make His will your priority. How real is your faith? Do you really follow Christ? Have you died to Him? Have you transformed? Are you saved? I know this sounds harsh, but I must be real with you. You must be real with yourself. You must be real with your Christian brothers and sisters. To really live out your God-given purpose, it must take priority over everything else—no exceptions, no excuses. God must come before family, before your career, before money, before hobbies, and before your personal desires.

The Secret

Here is the secret. If you place God no. 1, you will be better at everything else in life. You will be a better spouse and better parent, a better employee on the job, you will treat people better, you will do more "good" with your money, and you will enjoy life more. However, all that is still *not* your purpose. Your purpose is to *serve God*! You can do it amid all those things, but most Christians do it as an afterthought if it is convenient. They are busy with life. It is all too prevalent especially with American Christians. We are probably the busiest people on earth, and we typically only serve or give when it is convenient to do so. If God is the priority, you will serve God by doing your God-given purpose, and all the rest will follow.

I had a pastor once tell me to call your spouse as your no. 2 and have your spouse say that you come second in her life. The one who comes first is God. The most important relationship in my life is God. The most important relationship in my wife's life is God. It is more important for me to serve God than to serve her, and it is more important for her to serve God than to serve me. God obviously has roles for both (Ephesians 5:21–33; Colossians 3:18–19). But not before God. God makes me a better husband; I fail most every time on my own anyways. So God must be my no. 1, and my God-given purpose that He has for me must be my no. 1 priority because I am following Him. Plus, the most important part of my identity is God. Being with God is my eternal destination. I can lose everything else. In the end, it is me and God.

Culture teaches something completely different as we have explained in the last chapter. American culture always has a husband placing his wife first, and most wives expect to be first. What about everything else? Ask culture, and they will tell you everyone's purpose in life is happiness. But that is part of the problem in so many areas of our culture. God simply does not come first. You name the social issue, and you will find God absent from the equation. God must be first in our equation. We only remain on the face of this earth to serve our God-given purpose. But that too shall end.

"Trust in the Lord with all your heart and lean not on your own understanding; in all your ways submit to him, and he will make your paths straight" (Proverbs 3:5–6 NIV).

How to Find Your God-given Purpose

I promised at the beginning of the chapter I would tell you how to find your God-given purpose. This will take commitment, dedication, and perseverance to get through these. Then you must make your purpose a priority before God. No holding back. Your life must change. You must be transformed from whatever dreams and plans you have to the purpose that God has for you. If you already know your purpose, make it your top priority. If you do not, then here is how you find out:

- *Prayer.* Pray repeatedly and desperately for God to reveal His purpose for your life. Promise you will do it. Not your will but His will be done.

  "I cry out to God Most High, to God who fulfills his purpose for me" (Psalm 57:2 NIV).

- *His Word.* Read your Bible and search for God's Word about your purpose, and it will be revealed to you.

  "All Scripture is God-breathed and is useful for teaching, rebuking, correcting, and training in righteousness, so that the servant of God may be thoroughly equipped for every good work" (2 Timothy 3:16–17 NIV).

- *Be faithful.* Your faith will be tested, and you will face storms. The principalities of darkness do not want you to be transformed to God's purpose. But if you remain faithful, God will raise you up.

  "Well done, good and faithful servant! You have been faithful with a few things; I will put you in charge of many things. Come and share your master's happiness" (Matthew 25:21 NIV).

- *Evaluate strengths/gifts.* Your whole life has been a journey to prepare and equip you, even if unknowingly. You have certain things you are good at. Ask yourself and even write them down. Chances are, you will use those in His purpose.

  "Each of you should use whatever gift you have received to serve others, as faithful stewards of God's grace in its various forms" (1 Peter 4:10 NIV).

- *Include family.* You need family support, but you also have responsibility to spiritually lead them, which includes not only your spouse but also your children. This may mean you have to proclaim it if you are not there today. Plus, you will have to show you are serious. Your family may need time for them to see you transform. But you must proclaim boldly the following verse:

"As for Me and My Household, We Will Serve the Lord" (Joshua 24:15 NIV).

- *Start serving*. While you are waiting for God to reveal your God-given purpose, just start serving others. Find a need and be a blessing to them. It may be revealed after you make the first step. Remember my story. I had to start serving before I fully realized what God was telling me.

  "For we are his workmanship, created in Christ Jesus for good works, which God prepared beforehand, that we should walk in them" (Ephesians 2:10 NIV).

- *Church involvement.* This is not simply going to church, which is obvious. This means getting your church involved to help you. Inform your pastor and get elders/deacons, leaders, and fellow Christians to pray for you during this time. Seek their counsel.

  "So, Christ himself gave the apostles, the prophets, the evangelists, the pastors and teachers, to equip his people for works of service, so that the body of Christ may be built up" (Ephesians 4:11–12 NIV).

Be patient, weather the storms, and have faith that the Lord will reveal His God-given purpose for you. For those who know your purpose, be more deliberate and intentional about it. It is our responsibility to also help others find their purpose. It is part of making a disciple.

Focus on Your God-given Purpose

Remember that your God-given purpose is your reason for living. You will still have time to enjoy life, have fun, spend time with family and friends, work, and do life. But we must always remain diligent to our real purpose for this life. It is on serving God, and that requires focus. Once it is revealed to you, it is best to write it down and pray over a strategy of what it looks like. Remember my story above. I only shared it to support the points of this chapter. When God revealed to me that my God-given purpose was to minister to military and to first responders, I still had to organize it. I had to define what that looked like, set goals and objectives, and start forming tasks that needed to be accomplished. That plan had to be shaped, molded, and required God's intervention.

<u>Important Notes for Your Strategic Plan</u>:

• **God's plans are intentional.**	**They are deliberate and "bear fruit."**
• **God's plans are enduring.**	**They are not an isolated event**
• **God's plans bring people to Him.**	**Leads to people being saved/baptized**
• **God's plan is to make disciples.**	**Developing people is an investment and takes time**
• **God's plans requires others.**	**Get others involved- it is not about you (you are the servant)**
• **God's plans always change lives.**	**Most often one person at a time**

Who are your people? When Moses received his God-given purpose in the wilderness, it was to free God's people from Egypt, but they were also his people. He spent the rest of his life serving his people. For me, I consider veterans and first responders my people. That is who I serve, and that is who I pray for. I may volunteer to help other ministries, but I am clear on who my people are. I can get somewhat skeptical when people, churches, and organizations have a vision to change the world. I think it needs to be more realistic. Many of them are not even making changes around them. If they can focus on their people, they would be far more effective. You must know who you are specifically going to serve. When in doubt, you need to go back to the section above and "find your God-given purpose." It is important to get it right. In the military, we called understanding the 5Ws (who, what, where, when, and why) to be an important thing to communicate before taking on a new task. The "who" is your people. So let us go over an example of the 5Ws, and I will use me as an example.

Who: Veterans and first responders (my people)

What: Serve Ministries Inc. (SMI) with the mission to make disciples by creating chaplains to minister to veterans, first responders, and their families.

When: Daily for administration of SMI, Mondays for meetings. NPD Chaplain: Tuesday evening and Saturday morning (plus emergencies or when needed). Veterans: Wednesday evening and Sunday afternoon after church (plus when needed). I allow room for flexibility the rest of the week to respond to needs.

Where: Northwest Florida area (primarily Niceville)

Why: To fulfill my God-given purpose. To make disciples, which fulfills the Great Commission by creating volunteer and professional chaplains to serve in our community to meet the needs of physical, psychological/emotional, social, and spiritual wounds to ease the hurting, ensure they get healing, and are equipped to help others (H3 cycle). To lead those who have not been led to Christ and then make disciples of them. To ensure I am making a positive impact on the lives of those who are/were impacted from their service.

It is rather simple for me to rattle off the 5Ws because I have gone through the process to find my God-given purpose, and I know who my people are. The journey is very fluid and changing but spirit-led. I have a staff that is always assessing how we can positively make an impact on the veterans and first responders in our community. But I would like to provide a few examples of what a God-given purpose looks like and what I see many Christians doing when it comes to serving. There are many people who are volunteering, and there is nothing wrong with that. The world needs more people doing volunteer work. But volunteer work sometimes lacks a strategic plan, and it may not necessarily be your purpose.

Here are a few examples:

- *Serving in a church.* Many people start off serving in a church. Is this just volunteering time, or is this your God-given purpose? How can you tell? If you are the pastor, staff member, band member, or worship leader with the "calling" on your life that this position is your ministry, then it probably is. If you are handing out a program for a church event or handing out a bottle of water at a fair with your church's name on it, it is probably not. That is serving in a volunteer capacity, and it is good, but it is not your God-given purpose. Evaluate what you are currently doing with the important notes for a strategic plan above.

- *Mission trips*. Many people have a heart to do missions trips. Most will tell you that this is their God-given purpose. Is it? Do you have a defined strategic plan for it? If you have done them before, evaluate them and ask what God's plan was for those people. Far too many people go on a one- to two-week trips and serve as a volunteer, but that hardly counts as a God-given purpose. If God is "calling" you to do missions trips to [name the location/country], then that is your lifelong area of responsibility, your people, and your purpose. You will go there every opportunity you have. You may volunteer to do other things with your church and in your community at home. But your God-given purpose is the people in the area you are called. That means you are communicating with them all the time, developing strong relationships, assessing needs, and repeatedly going back there to be with your people. Lives will be changed, people saved, and disciples made. I have met many people who use mission trips as a travel club. I have met many who make comments that serving was more for them than the ones they were serving. It is nice to hear they got something out of it, but you were there to serve them, not yourself. God's plan will develop you, but serving God is not self-service. You can tell if this trip is a club or your purpose by whether you are committed to those people long-term. When in doubt, look at the list again above.
- *Missionaries*. These people just amaze me. They pack up their family and move to a new country to minister to the people there. They are in it for thc long haul, and it is most likely their God-given purpose for either or both spouses but probably a nice cultural and educational experience for their children. The need for a strategic plan remains. Did

you just move to a foreign country, or are you really living out your purpose? Most I have met are living out their purpose, but having a strategic plan may bring greater fidelity to ministering to the people God has placed in your trust.

- *Ministries*. I love ministries because they are usually led by someone who wants to make a difference and can usually find others who want to get involved. Some are through the local church (children's ministry, productions ministry, homeless ministry, worship ministry, etc.) Those I would lump into the category of serving in the church above, and this can be your God-given purpose. The ministries I am talking about here are nonprofit organizations external to the church to meet a community need. Serve Ministries Inc. (SMI) is one of those ministries. We work with many churches, ministries, and corporations to help minister to veterans and first responders. There are many start-ups, but many of them come and go or never really get established to begin with. Many of them do not become anything more than a glorified small group or Bible study. It is important to identify, What need is this ministry for? Who are my people? Why is this ministry important to the community? What do you do that churches are not doing (your ministry niche)? Have a strategic plan.

You have been called by God! If you still do not know what your purpose is, keep repeating this chapter and stay within the "find your God-given purpose" section. When ministering to others, use that section to guide people to find their purpose. Remember back to the H3 cycle. You are in the helping stage with a disciple now. You are helping them as part of your "helping" in the H3 cycle so they can perform their "helping" in their cycle. Once we come in agreement with God and start serving in our God-given purpose, we will have the ultimate fulfillment in life and have a glorious impact and the blessing to see lives change.

"Even as the Son of Man came not to be served but to serve, and to give his life as a ransom for many" (Matthew 20:28 NIV).

Application Questions

1. Do you know your God-given purpose? If not, then you may need to work in this chapter a while. If so, are you doing it?
2. Are you discouraged from fully engaging your God-given purpose by storms that have come in your life?
3. Can you have both money and ministry? What should we be cautious about?
4. What are some common excuses you hear about why people do not serve God? Are you guilty of any of them?
5. What is the real "secret" to your purpose in life?
6. Do you think the section on finding your God-given purpose is helpful to you and would be helpful to those you will minister to? Why?
7. What do you think are the most important aspects of having a strategic plan for your purpose?

***Once your God-given purpose is revealed, write it down. Write out your 5Ws and develop your strategic plan in writing. Share it with a pastor or mentor you can trust. Then get going, remain in prayer, and start serving!

CHAPTER 9

BODY-SOUL-SPIRIT

May God himself, the God of peace, sanctify you through and through. May your whole spirit, soul and body be kept blameless at the coming of our Lord Jesus Christ.

—1 Thessalonians 5:23

It is time to take a deeper look within. This is a time to see, really see, who we are and what we are made of. The truth and the reality are not a set of perceptions. Some people say, "Perceptions are reality," but I say that "perceptions are not always truth regardless if someone says it is their reality." I used to say that "a perception is a lazy man's excuse to finding truth." I changed it up, so it is a little more palatable for the easily offended. In a society where there are so many different views, different perspectives, and different perceptions, it is often hard to wade through the fake news to find truth. I want you to notice the title of this chapter, "Body-Soul-Spirit." We need to get to the truth of who we are. We must know so we can counter all the views, perspectives, and perceptions out there. Many people will tell you that what I am about to tell you is not the case. Some will give you a distorted perception, but we need to focus on the truth. We are a trichotomy of the body, soul, and spirit if we know Christ. We are a dichotomy (body and soul) otherwise.

The title of this book is *Spiritual Battleground*, which is the ultimate battle of good versus evil taking place over your soul. You are your soul; your soul is you! I often say, "Your soul is who is looking out of your eyeballs." Your body is just your "vehicle" for a little while before it is no longer functional. Your body will ultimately break down to the point it is unrepairable, and then you will die. Your soul is enduring, which theologically (the truth) will end up with God (in heaven) or without God (in hell). The target of both good and evil forces is the soul, and only one side will be victorious over it when the body fails. If you do not know Christ, Satan wins your soul. If you do know Christ, He owns your soul. As Christians, you know the only way to heaven is through Jesus Christ. That is the truth!

"I am the way and the truth and the life. No one comes to the Father except through me. If you really know me, you will know my Father as well" (John 14:6–7 NIV).

The Debate

The secular debate is not much of a debate at all. It is more of about accepting different views without the knowledge that any of them are correct or any of them getting to the truth. The secular perception is that you can establish your own truth and that we are all expected to accept that whatever someone believes is their truth. Secular views are fine without an absolute truth. You may have heard the phrase *mind, body, and soul.* It makes me cringe when I hear Christians say it and especially when I hear it in church. This is a very secular concept that is not completely inaccurate for nonbelievers, so let me explain. Just do a simple Google search on *mind, body, and soul*, and you will see many secular views for healthy living. Yet many secular, nonbelieving people, are predominately unsure about the idea of having a soul. Although some might like the notion that our soul lives on after we pass from this life, the views on what happens vary greatly. Others like the notion of having a spirit, some even claim to be spiritual people, but that does not exist outside of God. Some people completely reject the notion of a soul or spirit and that we are simply just human beings (monism). What is the truth? We will cover that shortly.

The theological debate is a little more complex of a debate based on biblical interpretation. Some biblical scholars hold to the view that we are a dichotomy, meaning we are made up of two parts (body and soul/spirit) based on the interpretation that soul and spirit are used interchangeably in the Bible. While others hold more of a trichotomy view or three parts (body, soul, and spirit), I happen to be convinced beyond a doubt that we are a trichotomy if we know Christ. For simple reference, see below:

Monism—secular view; one part (body)
Dichotomy—two parts (body and soul/spirit)
Trichotomy—three parts (body, soul, and spirit)

There is significant compelling biblical evidence to support the trichotomy position. I am usually surprised when I run into pastors who hold a dichotomy view. I understand how they reach this position, but if they will listen, I will share with them truth through the Bible. It is important to discuss this in order to understand what the target is for spiritual warfare, how we are susceptible to evil, how we can fall into darkness, and how the Holy Spirit is essential in cleaning our soul and having a relationship with God. The very premise of this discussion is a realization that there is a distinct difference between your soul and your spirit (if you have one).

"For the word of God is alive and active. Sharper than any double-edged sword, it penetrates even to dividing soul and spirit, joints and marrow (body); it judges the thoughts and attitudes of the heart" (Hebrews 4:12 NIV).

As you can see by the above verse, the Word of God tells us that we have a divided soul and spirit—two distinct parts. It also speaks of the heart; you have two. You have a physical heart that pumps blood through your body and a heart that is in your soul. Attitudes (personality and emotions) and thoughts (mind and intellect) are all part of your soul. We will cover this more in a bit.

The very challenge between dichotomy and trichotomy, I believe, has Darwinism roots. Those who believe in Darwinism would primarily side with the notion of monism; we live, and then we die as all living things do on earth. But there are many Darwinists who leave open the notion that we have souls but will make an argument that animals do as well. They base with argument on feelings and that animals have them too. Even theologians say that the soul is where are feelings come from. Animals can feel, love, have relationships, and mourn, which are all experiences that we attach to having a soul. Are they wrong? No! Animals do have souls, and they too will have an afterlife, but they do not have a spirit. We will explain this more when we explore the fascinating aspects of who we are.

I have also heard some theologians compare us as trinity being (trichotomy—body, soul, and spirit) because God is a trinity being (Father, Son, and Spirit). They make the argument that we were made in His image, which obviously comes from Genesis 1:27: "So God created mankind in his own image, in the image of God he created them; male and female he created them" (NIV). But the argument is flawed. There is no direct correlation between the parts to show a correlating "image" in this case. Although it is true that we were made in His image, we are not three persons in one. We have the potential for three parts. Most people only live with two (body and soul), just like animals. I hold to the trichotomy position based on Hebrews 4:12 and 1 Thessalonians 5:23 if you know Jesus Christ. This obviously needs more explanation.

You can also find several well-known preachers who have created models to show the body, soul, and spirit. When you finish reading this chapter, you will be more equipped to analyze each of them and find the flaws in some of them. There are many that are way off, but there are a few that I think blend a thorough understanding of biblical knowledge and what we know about our bodies. They even consider observations and analysis of studying animals. I unfortunately do not think a single model completely represents the truth. However, I will make my case for a new model and provide biblical references to justify each aspect. Therefore, I propose the following model as a proponent of the trichotomy position:

Trichotomy (Body, Soul, and Spirit)

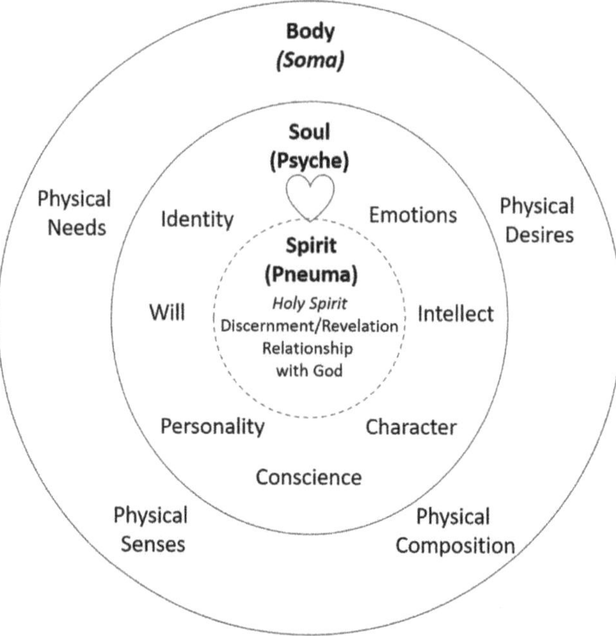

The Body

The body (*Soma*) consists of your five senses (see, hear, touch, smell, and taste) using your physical composition of the flesh (bones, skin, blood, organs, DNA, brain, heart, cells, etc.). It also contains your physical needs (food, water, clothing, shelter, sleep, oxygen, etc.). We also have physical desires (hunger, thirst, sex, physical activity, etc.). We generally know what the human body is, and regardless of one's views, we can all come to a consensus that we have a body. We can universally agree that we need to take care of our body for a higher quality of living and to prolong life. It can become disabled. It will eventually die. We see evidence to it day-to-day, and we do not see anyone defying death (physically). Sometimes you hear this in Christian circles as the "flesh," but that is out of context. The term *flesh* in Christianity refers to physical desires and therefore is not a complete description of our body.

The Soul

The soul (psyche) is a little more complicated, and it is the very essence of who you are. This is you! As mentioned before, this is who is looking out of your eyeballs. Your soul contains your identity, your character, your personality, your emotions, your feelings, and your passions. It also contains the heart of your soul. It is where your intellect, mind, thoughts, will, desires, imagination, reason, affections, and conscience (right and wrong) are located. Everyone has a soul, even animals. Animals just do not have all aspects of their soul as completely developed as humans, especially when it comes to intellect. So when you hear about a debate about us being no different than animals because they have all these things, they are not entirely incorrect. Biologists, zoologists, ethologists, psychologists, and others in the scientific community have conclusive evidence to support this position. They are all correct, and now you know why. It is because humans and animals all have a soul. Pet lovers may be happy to hear we all will exist after this life. Where they end up is God's decision that I do not profess to know.

Humans, however, are very distinctly different than animals. We are self-aware; our intellect is of a higher order. We can be creative, artistic, passionate, inventive, and analytical; we can experiment, and more. No other species has been able to do what a human being can do. That is not by some form of evolutionary accident or mistake. That is by design by God, within our soul, within our mind and our intellect. Not that it evolved that way but because it was designed that way. It was designed that way for a purpose—a purpose that has perplexed secular society. I am not suggesting that animals do not have a purpose, but they do not have a spiritual purpose. Humans were specifically designed to have a spiritual purpose. Even though humans were designed this way, many do not end up having a spirit in their soul, not a godly one anyways.

This is where it is important to note that an evil spirit(s) can and often do exist in the soul. We read about all the examples in the Bible of demonic spirits in Jesus's times. Where did they go, and why are spirits not being driven out today like Jesus and the disciples did during that time? I think it is because Christians are not given the supernatural power to draw out spirits today. But evil spirits still very much exist in the world. Look around, and you will find evil everywhere. Every evil act that humanity has ever done has come from the soul, driven by an evil spirit. Demonic spirits live in the soul. This is also why it is so easy for us to recognize when someone is evil. We see or hear of what they do, and we have an ability within our soul to recognize it as evil. They have been captivated by an evil spirit, and their soul becomes evil in all the contents mentioned above if they give into evil or lose the battle to evil.

"And do not fear those who kill the body but cannot kill the soul. Rather fear him who can destroy both soul and body in hell" (Matthew 10:28 NIV).

Your soul is a constant battleground between evil spirits and your spirit (if you have one). That is where I use the term *spiritual battleground*, which is the name of this book. I also refer to it as the "ultimate" battleground. It is not where all spiritual warfare takes place, but it is where spiritual battles take place over your soul. Your soul will eventually give in to evil spirits without a spirit from God. The Holy Spirit is not only to save your soul but also to fight evil in your soul. When you come to know Christ, your soul is saved, but the battles continue. Why? Because Satan wants to make you to be combat ineffective to execute your God-given purpose. For us to become combat effective, we need the Holy Spirit fighting for us with our spirit to win the battles raging from within our soul. It will be a constant battle over combat effectiveness. It is no longer a battle for your soul once the Holy Spirit is involved. When you know Christ, the war is already won for your soul. But do not be fooled. Satan will still fight, and he fights dirty. He is, after all, the great deceiver. He fights within your soul by offering you your fleshly desires, your passions, your wants and your thirsts for power, for fame, for money, for what you may think is love. He will deceive you on the bases of your happiness, all to distract you from your purpose.

> "For what will it profit a man if he gains the whole world and forfeits his soul? Or what shall a man give in return for his soul?" (Matthew 16:26 NIV)

The Spirit

"Jesus answered, 'Very truly I tell you, no one can enter the kingdom of God unless they are born of water and the Spirit. Flesh gives birth to flesh, but the Spirit gives birth to spirit'" (John 3:5–6 NIV).

The spirit (pneuma) provides discernment between what comes from God and what comes from man. When you see Spirit with a capital *S*, we are referring to the Holy Spirit. A small *s* is used to refer to your spirit (which is born when you accept Christ) both biblically and in this chapter. Your spirit is a revelation of the existence of God that comes with the ability to communicate directly with God. Those who are "born again" are "born of the spirit" and therefore has that spirit come alive in them to know God. Those who do not believe in Christ never have a spirit come alive because it is never birthed and therefore will never know God. Those who believe know God, and they have a relationship with Him. As previously mentioned, this is what separates us from animals. Animals cannot ever know God because they are unable to have a spirit. Unfortunately, many people refuse to believe in God, and therefore, they will not have a living spirit in them.

"But a natural man does not accept the things of the Spirit of God, for they are foolishness to him; and he cannot understand them, because they are spiritually appraised" (1 Corinthians 2:14 NIV).

Our spirit needs the spirit (Holy Spirit). With the spirit, we can know and have a relationship with our creator. This gives us the faculties to have faith, to worship, to pray, and to *minister* to others as representatives of God. Our spirit is also a dwelling place for the Holy Spirit to direct our path and to help us communicate with God in prayer and to guide us in ministry. It is not enough just to know but important to have a relationship with God to carry out our God-given purpose.

"In the same way, faith by itself, if it is not accompanied by action, is dead. But someone will say, 'You have faith; I have deeds.' Show me your faith without deeds, and I will show you my faith by my deeds. You believe that there is one God. Good! Even the demons believe that—and shudder" (James 2:17–19 NIV).

Having a spirit has a dual purpose. To house the Holy Spirit and to cleanse the soul. With the help of the Holy Spirit, our identity is changed. Our spirit cleans up our character, our personality, our emotions, our feelings, and our passions. It transforms our intellect, our mind, our thoughts, our will for His will, our desires, and it impacts our conscience. The Holy Spirit works with our spirit to clean up our life and transform our identity.

"The Spirit himself testifies with our spirit that we are God's children" (Romans 8:16 NIV).

Our spirit also impacts our mind within our soul. But the free will of our soul is not taken away. We must actively have our spirit work with the Holy Spirit (by choice) to completely transform into who God wants us to be (body, soul, and spirit). The Holy Spirit will regenerate the body and the soul if we allow Him. Again, it must be by choice. God wants you to make that choice. That is why so many Christians are not transforming into what God wants them to be. They simply have not made that choice. It is because the free will of their soul is not permitting their spirit to transform their soul. That is also why we still sin after becoming a Christian. The evil of the soul is winning the battle over the mind.

"Do not conform to the pattern of this world but be transformed by the renewing of your mind. Then you will be able to test and approve what God's will is—his good, pleasing, and perfect will" (Romans 12:2 NIV).

As you can see from several verses now, there is a difference between our spirit and the Holy Spirit. They are not one and the same. Our spirit is part of us when it is birthed. The Holy Spirit is not. It is a "portion" for the lack of better terms of God, the third person of the Trinity. It is one of God's mysteries on exactly how He does it. But we are not God, and we do not become God by having it. We become "children of God" (changing our identity) and therefore can have a relationship with Him while still dealing with and fighting the battles within our soul.

"The mind governed by the flesh is death, but the mind governed by the Spirit is life and peace" (Romans 8:6 NIV).

Why do we need a spirit if we have a soul? That is a challenging question that we will answer here. As previously mentioned, evil resides in your soul. God designed a place where the Holy Spirit can reside. God cannot reside with evil. Evil cannot reside with God. So God gives a spirit for the Holy Spirit to reside in. Think of it as a secret compound (your spirit) within a larger base (your soul). There are those on the base who cannot get access to the secret compound, but the secret compound can impact and can make a base more powerful. This design allows your spirit to cleanse your soul and, with your free will, begin removing evil from your life. Your spirit belongs to God, and it is connected to your soul to transform it. Since our spirit is connected to your soul, God owns it, and therefore, this is what God brings home to him when you are completed with this life.

"And the dust returns to the earth as it was, and the spirit returns to God who gave it" (Ecclesiastes 12:7 NIV).

You probably figured out by now that the soul is very connected to the body. Your soul is who you are and will only be separated from the body after your physical death. Your soul and spirit will then be given a spiritual body, but that is a different topic for a different time. Your physical body contains your soul and can contain your spirit when you know Christ. Therefore, your body becomes a temple for the Holy Spirit when you accept God. At that point, your body and soul (and obviously your spirit) belong to God, and everything of who we are now belongs to Him.

"Or do you not know that your body is a temple of the Holy Spirit within you, whom you have from God? You are not your own, for you were bought with a price. So, glorify God in your body." (1 Corinthians 6:19–20 NIV).

It is time to get truly connected with your spirit. Take this to prayer, take this to worship, take this to fasting. Seek God, and He will give your spirit what you need to serve Him and know Him more.

"I keep asking that the God of our Lord Jesus Christ, the glorious Father, may give you a spirit of wisdom and revelation, so that you may know him better" (Ephesians 1:17 NIV).

Ministry Point

"For God gave us a spirit not of fear but of power and love and self-control" (2 Timothy 1:7 NIV).

To be effective in ministry, we must walk in the spirit. That means allowing the Holy Spirit to guide your path so you can serve. Our purpose is to serve God, plain and simple.

"But I say, walk by the Spirit, and you will not gratify the desires of the flesh. For the desires of the flesh are against the Spirit, and the desires of the Spirit are against the flesh, for these are opposed to each other, to keep you from doing the things you want to do" (Galatians 5:16–17 NIV).

We are not here to do the things we want to do; we are here to do what God wants us to do. It does not mean He will not bless us, and it does not mean we will not enjoy life. But we must not lose sight of our purpose. We are here to serve the spirit that comes from God, and this is where we get our strength to serve and the power to reframe from fleshly desires. If we are not serving, it is because we are not walking in the spirit, and we are not tapped into the power of our spirit. But God gave us all this for us to use for His will. We do not need to be afraid to use it, for the Lord our God is with us.

"For God gave us a spirit not of fear but of power and love and self-control" (2 Timothy 1:7 NIV).

You might feel a little beat-up right now; I know I get that way. We come to the realization that we are living life for ourselves, and we are not living life for our God-given purpose. Your initial thoughts are probably intense. You may think your life needs a complete overhaul. It seems like a lot of work. Well, I am here to tell you that you are correct. We cannot have our life and His life for us simultaneously; one will always give way to the other through our choices. This is where we must pick up our cross. It is a hardcore reality that is essential for ministry. Jesus said, "Whoever wants to be my disciple must deny themselves and take up their cross daily and follow me" (Luke 9:23 NIV).

You probably heard and read this verse many times before. Most of us focus on the word *cross*, and rightfully so. What Jesus did on the cross is everything, and I mean everything, to us. To follow Him, though, means that we are willing to die to self to serve. But I would like to point out a different word—the word *daily*—because we will be hit with life's challenges. The people around us have souls, which sometimes are being dominated by evil spirits. They will give you responsibilities, have expectations, and place demands on your life daily that will get in the way. Some will and may be innocent, many are even needed, some knowingly or unknowingly intentional, and some simply demonically intended to distract you. Before you know it, days, weeks, months, and even years go by, and you are not serving, not living your purpose.

"I have been crucified with Christ and I no longer live, but Christ lives in me. The life I now live in the body, I live by faith in the Son of God, who loved me and gave himself for me" (Galatians 2:20 NIV).

I would further suggest people really are not living much at all without the Holy Spirit. They are existing, but they are not living. How many of you are people watchers? I must admit that I am. My view of watching people changed when my life transformed into ministry. I started seeing people in a different way. I started seeing "lost" people. I started seeing these lost people as just existing. I saw people existing at work, in the airport, at the store, and throughout the community. Even people whom I know were essentially living day-to-day without purpose and striving to find a way to be happy. People trying to buy their way into happiness, changing relationships to find happiness, trying new activities to find happiness, and working hard to afford happiness. Everyone is on the "go" but sadly are just existing, living the proverbial "circle of life" day after day. Ironically, most of them are not happy. Until you connect with the Holy Spirit in your spirit and live according to God's will, you will be existing, and you really will not experience true life.

"Jesus said, 'The Spirit gives life; the flesh counts for nothing. The words I have spoken to you—they are full of the Spirit and life'" (John 6:63 NIV).

Parting Notes

As we depart from this chapter, I want to leave you with this. Glorify God that you have a spirit and that you have the Holy Spirit living within you. Allow your spirit to fight the evil desires of your soul. Remember your God-given purpose and live your life according to His will. Fight the good fight! Worship and remain in the truth.

If we find ourselves feeling disconnected from God, it is time for prayer and time for worship. It may be our fleshly desires getting in the way due to sin brought about by evil spirits in our soul. When that happens, it is time to deny the flesh, combat the soul, and connect with the spirit; it is time for fasting. Fasting is a perfect time to focus on the spirit. It is a deliberate engagement in battle that intensifies cleaning of the soul. Fast often so the Holy Spirit can break down fleshly barriers.

"'Even now,' declares the Lord, 'return to me with all your heart, with fasting and weeping and mourning'" (Joel 2:12 NIV).

Stay within the Word of God and stay true to your God-given purpose.

"Anyone who listens to the word but does not do what it says is like someone who looks at his face in a mirror and, after looking at himself, goes away and immediately forgets what he looks like. But whoever looks intently into the perfect law that gives freedom and continues in it—not forgetting what they have heard but doing it—they will be blessed in what they do" (James 1:23–25 NIV).

Review/Application Questions

1. Where is the spiritual battleground within you and explain how both good and evil can be fighting within and over it?
2. Do animals have a soul? Explain. How would you answer if someone asks whether their pet is going to heaven?
3. Do you believe we are made up of a trichotomy (three parts—body, soul, and spirit) or dichotomy (two parts—body and soul/spirit)? Why?
4. What is our psyche, and what is it comprised of?
5. What is the purpose of your spirit?
6. Does the Holy Spirit exist in your soul? Explain why or why not.
7. What do we need to do if we are not executing our God-given purpose?

CHAPTER 10

GUILTY OF FALLING SHORT

For all have sinned and fall short of the glory of God.
—Romans 3:23 NIV

For those of you who have been in ministry for some time, you have ministered to people who are not saved. Sometimes you must work with them for some time while the Holy Spirit works on them. Hopefully, you can see the Holy Spirit working on their lives and see that moment where you can tell they are ready to accept Him. You share the gospel message, perhaps using the Roman's road to salvation, and you can visibly see it impacting them. You hear them respond, and you are humbly given the honor to lead them to our savior, Jesus Christ. For the individual, part of that conviction is the realization that they have sinned against a perfect God and that they have "fallen short" of His perfect standard. But through His grace, they are forgiven based on what Jesus did on the cross. Of course, He is the only way (John 14:6). Everyone reading this book should know that.

However, Christians still sin and fall short of God's glory regularly. As you are aware, sin does not instantaneously go away after someone is saved. We can see plenty of these examples, and there are many reasons for this. The primary reason has to do with free will.

Evil spirits are still holding the soul captive with sin. The next reason is that they must go through a transformational period (Romans 12:2). This may be due to not getting rid of a sin in life after salvation. It may simply be the sin of not following God's commandment to make disciples (Matthew 28:19–20). In other cases, the person may mean well but are making errors while still in the process of their transformation. Even mature Christians can still fall short with an altercation with a spouse, an emotional reaction to a coworker, or ignoring God's calling on them to intervene in someone's life. Think through your life. Have there been times when you stumbled? Do you think you are doing everything right all the time and without error that God wants you to do?

"The LORD directs the steps of the godly. He delights in every detail of their lives. Though they stumble, they will never fall, for the LORD holds them by the hand" (Psalm 37:23–24 NIV).

Chances are, we stumble on our God-given purpose (discussed in chapter 8) and therefore fall short of the glory of God. Let us face it, we all have, and we all do. In this reality, it would be easy to throw your hands up and give up. Billy Graham was interviewed before he died and was asked what he thinks about meeting with Jesus. He replied, and I am paraphrasing, that he was concerned that he fell short of what God wanted him to do. When I first heard of this, I was shocked! If Billy Graham was concerned after all people he led to Christ, after the clear visible proof that he was living out his God-given purpose, and the global reach he had as being one of the most influential Christian speakers of all time, what hope is there for any of us? But he humbly wondered if he had done all that he was tasked by our Lord to do. For Billy Graham, his time on earth was running out, and he contemplated whether he fully completed the Lord's work. Did he feel that he fell short in the end? It seems so. What is our assessment of ourselves? Billy Graham is with Jesus now, and I am sure he heard those words we all want to hear from Christ—"Well done, good and faithful servant" (Matthew 25:21 NIV). I do not think it is something we need to beat ourselves up about. We should simple stay "within the Lord" and do the best we can. But we need to try to stay on target.

Being On-target

I propose that falling short is a part of Christian living. I compare this to target practice. As veterans and law enforcement officers, we shoot on the range so we can get more on-target, more proficient, and to hit the bull's-eye more routinely. Although we cannot be perfect every time we shoot, we strive to improve and to tighten our shot group. We desire to hit the bull's-eye regularly. We even dream about shooting the perfect score when we go to the range. Then we see where the rounds land when we get there and mostly fall short of our own expectation when we see the results. However, we know if we can achieve an "Expert" rating, it can translate into more efficiency in an engagement where our life is often on the line. We know we are far more effective in combat if we can hit the targets we are shooting at. The same goes for Christian living and serving in our God-given purpose. We will not always hit the bull's-eye, but we should eagerly strive and even pray to be as close to the bull's-eye of our God-given purpose as often as we can. Other people's lives are on the line. Being an expert shooter in our purpose does not happen by accident. It takes dedication, commitment, and perseverance. We must work at it.

What Does Your Target Look Like?

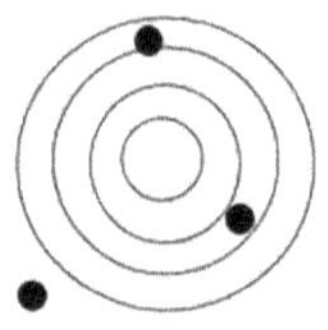

Unable to Remain On-Target
Erratic, all over the place
Shaken Faith
Purpose Unclear

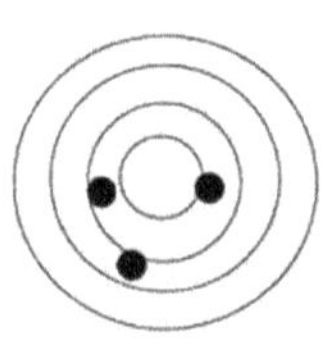

Routinely On-Target
Inconsistent Persistence
Has Firm Faith
Still Defining Purpose

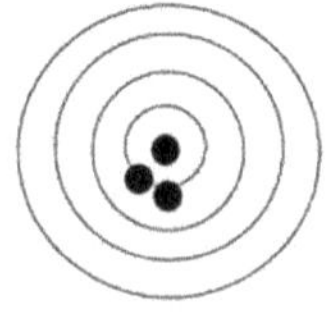

Tight Shot-Group
Consistent Persistence
Strong in the Faith
Living God-Given Purpose

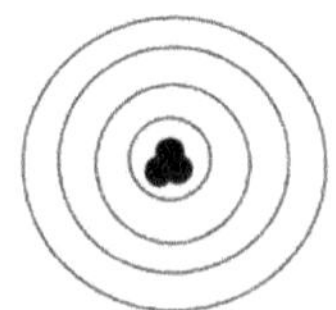

Bulls-eye Precision
Passionate Daily
Unshakable Faith
Unstoppable in
God-Given Purpose

Most of us go to the range to qualify on our weapon. You can be assured that you have already qualified to serve God if you have accepted Christ. Great news! We are qualified, and He commands that we serve, and He is with us every step of the way. Do not allow anyone to tell you that you are not qualified. There are many "Pharisees" wanting to disqualify you. There are many demons that will point to all your imperfections to discourage you. There are people all around you who will try to tear you down, even family members and friends. They all remember those moments when you did not do something right in life. They remember all your failures, all your dark moments, and many of the times you sinned. You must stand firm and tell them who you are now. Even a new believer in Christ can turn around and help lead his/her friend to Christ instantaneously without knowing really anything other than what Jesus means to them and why they were saved. A person's testimony on how they came to know Christ is a powerful ministry tool.

In this marksmanship illustration, it is about perfecting your tradecraft. You do not simply want to shoot rounds downrange; you want to be an expert, hitting the bull's-eye often. Unlike shooting, it is not about technique; it is more about your heart condition. Are you in tune with the Holy Spirit, with your spirit, and with what is going on in your soul (the heart of your soul)? We went over this in the last chapter. Are you in a position in your walk with the Lord where you are unable to remain on-target? Does your service to God seem erratic, and do you feel you are just all over the place? Has your faith been shaken? Are you unclear about your purpose? If so, do you think it is about time you fix this and improve in your marksmanship? Obviously, we want to move to the point where we have bull's-eye precision. We are passionate about serving the Lord daily, we have unshakable faith, and we feel unstoppable in our God-given purpose.

For about 80 percent of Christians, their target is one of the first two in the figure above. Some church leaders would probably argue the number is above 90 percent. Surprisingly, most of my ministry is not counseling the unsaved but counseling people who already profess to be a Christian. I will say 80–90 percent of them are on one of the first two targets. It may be surprising to know, but I would say most of them are really on the first target. Why do you think that is? I believe it is because people are not investing in their discipleship. There are also few people making disciples. So many Christians simply are not developing in their faith. The crazy reality is that most Christians are disobedient because God wants all Christians to make disciples. We have heard about the Great Commission. We know it is God's will, but little is done to execute it. The hard reality is that most have not, do not, and will not.

Falling Short on Sharing the Good News

According to LifeWay Research, about 55 percent of Christians pray monthly about sharing their faith with someone. However, only 45 percent of Christians have shared their faith in the past six months.[49] An even more shocking statistic according to Bible.org suggests 95 percent of Christians have never led anyone to Christ.[50] So if you hold both studies to be true, most of the 45 percent of Christians out there sharing their faith are not leading anyone to Christ. Why is this? Simply put, there is a difference between sharing your faith with someone and engaging someone else about their faith. Certainly, it is good to share your "testimony" and how Jesus has made an impact in your life. But that cannot be all to the conversation. The conversation must transition to the other person (it cannot be all about you), and I think this is where so many people struggle and fall short.

"For I am not ashamed of the gospel, because it is the power of God that brings salvation to everyone who believes: first to the Jew, then to the Gentile" (Romans 1:16 NIV).

One of my favorite classes in seminary was a class I took with Dr. David Wheeler one of the times I took leave and did a class at Liberty University. He taught the class on evangelism, and I recall absorbing every word he spoke. He was a very engaging teacher, and I

---

49 LifeWay Research. April 23, 2019. "Evangelism More Prayed for Than Practiced by Churchgoers." Retrieved from the web at https://lifewayresearch.com/2019/04/23/evangelism-more-prayed-for-than-practiced-by-churchgoers/ on May 28, 2020. Discipleship Pathway Assessment—Sharing Christ: Representative Survey of Protestant Churchgoers.

50 Bible.org. "Evangelism Statistics." Retrieved from https://bible.org/illustration/evangelism-statistics on May 28, 2020.

was excited about the topic. He also used a required reading that was not a scholarly textbook but still very impactful. It was a book called *Share Jesus Without Fear* by William Fay. I highly recommend getting it. He proposes five questions that you must share with someone[51]:

1. Do you have any kind of spiritual belief?
2. Who is Jesus to you?
3. Do you believe there is a heaven or a hell?
4. If you died tonight, where do you think you would go? If heaven, why?
5. If what you believe were not true, would you want to know?

William Fay then provides scriptures to use to lead them through their understanding of what God says about sin and why they need a savior. I particularly like how he has the person read each verse and then asks, "What does this say to you?" If they stumble on giving the correct answer, he tells them to "read it again" until they give a correct answer. This has been a technique I have used for the past twelve years. The only difference is that I use the "Romans Road to Salvation" instead of the verses he proposes, but I still have the other person read them.

The Romans Road to Salvation

"For all have sinned, and come short of the glory of God" (Romans 3:23 NIV).

"For the wages of sin is death; but the gift of God is eternal life through Jesus Christ our Lord" (Romans 6:23 NIV).

"But God demonstrates his own love for us in this: While we were still sinners, Christ died for us" (Romans 5:8 NIV).

---

[51] Fay, William. 1999. *Share Jesus Without Fear*. Nashville, Tennessee: B&H Publishing Group: p. 146.

"If you declare with your mouth, 'Jesus is Lord,' and believe in your heart that God raised him from the dead, you will be saved. For it is with your heart that you believe and are justified, and it is with your mouth that you profess your faith and are saved." (Romans 10:9–10 NIV).

- Administer a sinner's prayer (recommend using your own words).

"Everyone who calls on the name of the Lord will be saved" (Romans 10:13 NIV).

Here are a few additional recommendations:

1. Always have the Romans Road to Salvation on you. In today's day and age, we all have phones, and I have the Romans Road to Salvation saved as a picture I can easily pull up in my Notes app. I know others who have it printed out and folded in their wallet or their purse. I think your phone is the best option today. Practice pulling it up quickly so you are prepared when the Holy Spirit starts moving in someone's life. I can pull mine up in seconds. You want to be a reliable partner with the Holy Spirit.
2. Ensure you have them read the verses and ask them, just as William Fay suggests, What does it say to you? after they read each verse. Do not be afraid to ask them to "read it again" if they do not understand. Each verse is very straightforward, and the Holy Spirit will help.
3. I have the person repeat the sinner's prayer after me a few words at a time. I do not read it; I speak from my heart using the Holy Spirit. You should generally know what you need to say for a sinner's prayer, but I think it is more genuine and authentic if it is put in your own words.
4. After they are saved, I talk to them about baptism and invite them to church. Schedule a baptism with your pastor if you do not feel equipped to do it yourself. As a ministry leader or chaplain, ask to administer the baptism if it is

conducted at the church. You are not fully doing the Great Commission if you are not baptizing, so start preparing. Tell the person you will coordinate for their baptism and that you will decide on a date with them soon.

"And now what are you waiting for? Get up, be baptized and wash your sins away, calling on his name" (Acts 22:16 NIV).

5. Tell the person to share this news that they have accepted Jesus Christ as their Lord and savior with friends and family. Encourage them to invite friends and family to witness the baptism when it is scheduled. I feel this is especially important. The Bible talks about a public profession of faith. I believe this has purpose—it makes the new believer accountable and will begin the process of transformation from who they were to who God wants them to be. It will also be a launching point to tell people who witness that he/she is a representative of God now and that they have repented for their sins.

"In the same way, I tell you, there is rejoicing in the presence of the angels of God over one sinner who repents" (Luke 15:10 NIV).

Many people claim to be evangelists; I am not one of them. But I know I am commanded to do so. Even though this was my favorite class in seminary, I consider myself a chaplain. I administer to people's needs (their different types of wounds). When the opportune time presents itself to lead someone to Christ, I will and do so. As a chaplain, I consider my primary responsibility to meet their needs. My secondary responsibility is making disciples since most of the people I minister to are already Christians. My third responsibility is leading someone to Christ if they do not know Him. Do I fall short on leading people to Christ? Well, that depends on how you define success or falling short. My general assumption is that I do fall short in all three areas quite often, so I am constantly striving to seek self-improvement. By doing so, I think God uses me more. I generally feel I do a good job about discipleship making, but I may still be falling short when it comes to evangelism.

"But you, keep your head in all situations, endure hardship, do the work of an evangelist, discharge all the duties of your ministry" (2 Timothy 4:5 NIV).

Falling Short in Making Disciples

The Great Commission is often misunderstood, and I think this is causing many Christians to fall short. The lines are blurred between leading someone to Christ and making disciples. Part of the confusion may be with the translation of the verse, so I think it is important to discuss this to clarify and alleviate any confusion:

"Therefore, go and make disciples of all nations, baptizing them in the name of the Father and of the Son and of the Holy Spirit, and teaching them to obey everything I have commanded you. And surely, I am with you always, to the very end of the age" (Matthew 28:19–20 NIV).

The command is to "go" and make disciples, then it states to baptize them and teach them. The word *go* is emphasized by every pastor who preaches this verse. But this is where the average Christian gets stumped. So the Christian reads the verse again, and the questions start flowing in their minds. Is this what God is expecting us to do? Do I know how to make a disciple? Am I authorized to baptize someone? What if I do not know very much to teach someone else? If I am struggling with questions like these, how am I going to be obedient to this command by God? Pastors get frustrated because people are not going, and the people are frustrated because they do not know what to do.

So let us look at the verse more closely. It does not suggest making someone a disciple first, then baptize them before you teach them. Jesus is not laying out a chronological sequence of events by this statement. Instead, He wants a complete salvation experience of accepting Him and being baptized and then growing in the faith to become a disciple of Christ.

"Repent and be baptized every one of you in the name of Jesus Christ for the forgiveness of your sins, and you will receive the gift of the Holy Spirit" (Acts 2:38 NIV).

What I have found is that most Christians associate making a disciple as leading someone to Christ. This is further from the truth. In modern application, this means leading them to Christ, inviting them to church, and having the pastor baptize them. When this is done, it is then encouraged that they go to church regularly and ideally join a small group and volunteer within the church. All this is not bad; it is a good method. However, this approach still falls short. When we take this approach, I argue we are not making a disciple. We are spreading the gospel and getting them involved in church activities.

"Go into all the world and preach the gospel to all creation. Whoever believes and is baptized will be saved, but whoever does not believe will be condemned" (Mark 16:15–16 NIV).

This is another "go" verse to preach the gospel. This verse can also be confusing. Did you know that you are commanded to preach? For most, this means sharing the gospel message and leading someone to Christ. This does not necessarily mean you need to stand behind the pulpit. So do not feel bad if you are one of those people who have issues with stage fright. Actually, standing behind the pulpit is not fulfilling the "go" command as pastors are waiting for people to come to them in church. For a pastor and any other Christian, this verse refers to "going" out from the church and preaching the gospel within their community, the nation, and the world (their Jerusalem, Judea, and the ends of the earth). This is evangelism, which is distinctly different from discipleship making.

"But you will receive power when the Holy Spirit comes on you; and you will be my witnesses in Jerusalem, and in all Judea and Samaria, and to the ends of the earth" (Acts 1:8 NIV).

There is a *debate* that may be the root cause of Christians falling short in making disciples. The first issue is who was Jesus talking to in the Great Commission? If your answer is His disciples, you are correct! The debate is whether this command also applies to every Christian or just those "set apart" as his apostles to do the Lord's work. We know certain people are "set apart" to do the Lord's work.

"So Christ himself gave the apostles, the prophets, the evangelists, the pastors and teachers, to equip his people for works of service, so that the body of Christ may be built up until we all reach unity in the faith and in the knowledge of the Son of God and become mature, attaining to the whole measure of the fullness of Christ" (Ephesians 4:11–13 NIV).

I am sure many of you who have been in ministry for some time have read the above verse, but it is important to break this verse down to grasp the true meaning of it. Look at what God does with people He calls to be apostles, prophets, evangelists, pastors, and teachers. He calls them to equip people. For what purpose? It is to serve (works of service), so we can build one another up (the body of Christ) and make disciples (those who are mature and have the whole measure of the fullness of Christ).

The second part of the debate of the Great Commission is who is qualified to baptize people. This is a difficult subject because the Bible really does not specify. Church tradition tells us that those who are "set apart" as priests are to administer the baptism (and the Lord's Supper). However, the Bible makes no such declaration. If you read the verse that states, "You also, like living stones, are being built into a temple of the Spirit to be a holy priesthood, offering spiritual sacrifices acceptable to God through Jesus Christ" (1 Peter 2:5 NIV), then you can make an argument any disciple of Christ can baptize someone. There are verses that show that people are "set apart" to do the Lord's work (Acts 14:23, Romans 15:16, 1 Timothy 5:17, Titus 1:5, James 5:14–15), but they do not specifically declare those who are "set apart" as having the sole responsibility to baptize. Even John the Baptist appeared to be "set apart" with a God-given purpose to baptize, but he is the only scriptural example. Baptism is covered many times in the Bible with no emphasis on who was doing the baptizing (Acts 2:41; 8:12; 9:18; 10:48; 16:33; 18:8). The emphasis was always on the person being baptized. Even Paul only baptized a few people and preferably mostly taught. He was careful about baptizing because he did not want people to think he was exalting himself (1 Corinthians 1:14–17). I think it is important that the baptism is conducted scripturally sound and led by the Holy Spirit. The focus is on the person being baptized, not on who is administering it. But any disciple of Christ can do a baptism just like any disciple can make another disciple.

"...to be a minister of Christ Jesus to the Gentiles. He gave me the priestly duty of proclaiming the gospel of God, so that the Gentiles might become an offering acceptable to God, sanctified by the Holy Spirit" (Romans 15:16 NIV).

We are commanded to make disciples and baptize them. Leading someone to Christ is just the first step. Baptism is step 2. Encouraging them to attend church is probably a solid step 3. But making a disciple is so much more. It starts with the above three, but the unfortunate result is an immature Christian if that is all that is done. The result of an immature Christians is they, in turn, are not making disciples. They are deflecting that on the church for it to occur in Sunday services and deflecting it on other Christians in small groups. True discipleship making is an investment in the individual so they grow in the faith and therefore can lead others to Christ and make disciples of them. There are clear evidence when someone becomes a disciple that are visible. You are not finished making them a disciple until you see them leading others to Christ and developing others as disciples. I would still argue that you should still mentor them.

If you were to ask most Christians, they cannot explain how to make a disciple. There is a reason for this—they were never taught because nobody really made them a disciple. So the problem keeps manifesting itself. There is plenty of room for effective ministry in this area of making disciples because it is so poorly done around the world. I especially get excited about making disciples of veterans and first responders. They already know what it means to serve (it is already ingrained within their soul), and most of them are driven, hardworking, type A personalities who value the camaraderie of their fellow brothers and sisters in service. To me, they make powerful and impactful disciples for the kingdom. I personally would prefer three of these disciples than three thousand others who have never served. If we take the time to engage them and develop them (making them a disciple), they will be very impactful in the community and in any church. They most likely will be the difference makers.

Churches Falling Short

I am often amazed by how much pride a church has and how defensive people can get about their local church. Is the local church not simply a flock within the greater body of Christ? Are we all not supposed to be *one* body of Christ? It just goes to show you just how much "man" falls short and how amazing our perfect God is to even work with us. There are hundreds of denominations comprising the body of Christ, but we do not act like we are "one body" under the lordship of Christ and "of" Him. Which denomination is right? Why do so many disagree and "see" the scripture differently? Are denominations nothing more than interpretational differences of man and stylistic differences, with some draped with tradition? Even nondenomination churches end up having their own culture and their own belief system, develop their own traditions after a while, and become their own undeclared denomination. You can instantly tell in their start-up classes or by visiting their website because all churches usually start off with their faith statement and some comments that start with, "This is what we believe." They all tie their beliefs to the scripture. But they are not all the same. All these have man-made influence! I have studied so many of the denominations in seminary, and most all of them have dark histories or have and currently are falling short. What started off as a fascinating study ended up being rather repulsive. Those "called" to lead a church must be self-conscious of this.

"Keep watch over yourselves and all the flock of which the Holy Spirit has made you overseers. Be shepherds of the church of God, many manuscripts of the Lord which he bought with his own blood" (Acts 20:28 NIV).

Personally, I have an enormous amount of respect for the "elders" of the church. They have the hardest job in the world working for a boss that is perfect. People have high expectations of them, and they will fall short of meeting everyone's expectations. I think they deserve to have their place of honor. Unfortunately, many have not only fallen short but were also led by demonic spirits down dark paths into inexcusable sin. Still, those who are "truly called" by God have an immense responsibility. They are called to "tend to the flock" under their care. The majority are great at what they do.

"The elders who direct the affairs of the church well are worthy of double honor, especially those whose work is preaching and teaching" (1 Timothy 5:17 NIV).

Sunday services fall short! In American churches, most of the services are basic life application biblical messages to be better Christians laced with a "good news" message in the event someone showed up who is not saved. All this is great stuff, right? Well, even though his sounds good, there is a significant issue. Christians are called to do so much more than just live a good Christian life. Most Christians seem satisfied with this because it does not really challenge them to grow. Most do not want to evangelize, make disciples, or pursue their God-given purpose. They go to church, get a good life application message about being a good Christian, then they can go on their way and live another week of their life. Maybe once in a while, they give an offering, and perhaps, they will occasionally invite a friend to church. Less than 10 percent of Christians tithe, and less than 10 percent serve, and they are not always the same 10 percent. I hear so many pastors complain about getting their congregations to be more involved and serve our Lord. Behind the scenes, I have heard them complain people are not giving. I think this is something the pastor needs to take to the Lord to bring change.

It is the Lord who is the head of the church, but it is administered by a pastor who strives to lead this part of the body to the best of his ability, assuming his intentions are pure. Most churches have an altar call to lead nonbelievers who come to church that day, and most offer baptism services that can be scheduled for a later time. However, few offer any discipleship training. Without discipleship training, who is making disciples? How can a church expect their laity to make disciples if they were not trained, nor did they become disciples themselves? If you go back and review the statistics from the section on falling short on sharing the good news, the data therefore makes more sense on what problem exists. People do not know how to share the "good news," and they know even less about making disciples. In American churches, they do not think they are equipped to make disciples, nor do they think they have the authority to baptize anyone (reserved by tradition for those ordained to do one of the two sacraments: administering the Lord's Supper and baptisms). They also feel they do not know enough to teach. So how can anyone under these presuppositions and context fulfill the Great Commission?

Discipleship Training

My recommendation to churches is to establish a discipleship training program. To be clear, this is not the classes you give to new member prospects so they learn about your church, nor how to get them involved in the church, nor how to be a leader in your church in a missions area or of a small group. All churches have these introduction classes that build on the previous one. A discipleship program is more than a Bible study or a small group. It is a program specifically intended to grow a disciple in the faith with all the above as a baseline. So I am not suggesting taking anything away. I am only suggesting you add a discipleship training program focused primarily in three areas.

Discipleship training focus on three main areas:

1. How to share the "good news" and evangelize to someone and lead them to Christ. I have already provided the basics above in the section on falling short in sharing the good news.
2. How to baptize. This includes studying the biblical scriptures about this, which is briefly discussed in the section above on falling short in making disciples. This should include baptism practice to build confidence.
3. Giving them what they need to teach. Obviously start with the Bible. But this includes the essential elements on developing a new believer into a disciple. This includes expository Bible teaching, life application, church involvement, and discipleship training.

*** The circle of life includes the circle of the Great Commission

As a minister, pastor, chaplain, or any other disciple serving in any capacity, this is what I would recommend taking to the Lord in prayer. Ask the Lord for wisdom on how to fulfill the Great Commission and how you would implement a discipleship training program within your church (if one does not exist) or how you would implement one in your home.

Important for Ministry

"Do your best to present yourself to God as one approved, a worker who does not need to be ashamed and who correctly handles the word of truth" (2 Timothy 2:15 NIV).

For those who are or feel called to be by God to be "set apart" to serve in a church, ministry, or as a chaplain, I would like to impart of you a few important insights into the significance you have in the process of someone's eternal destination. First, remember who you represent—God. Present yourself accordingly and remain in the truth. You must never forget where you come from and what God-given purpose you are now charged with.

"But you are a chosen people, a royal priesthood, a holy nation, God's special possession, that you may declare the praises of him who called you out of darkness into his wonderful light" (1 Peter 2:9 NIV).

We have a mission to be ambassadors for Christ. We must represent Him to the best of our ability. Far too many who have come before us have made mistakes that have tarnished our calling. When we fall short, we must repent, seek forgiveness, and then we need to get back at it. We are forgiven, so we cannot let it consume us. We also must work harder because of all the horrible stories you hear about pastors and priests who have committed horrible sins. We will make mistakes too, but a mistake is distinctly different from a blatant sin. You know the difference. We must constantly strive to hit the bull's-eye of our God-given purpose. We need to remain in communication, in worship, in connection, in strength, and in good conscience with our God.

"We are therefore Christ's ambassadors, as though God were making his appeal through us. We implore you on Christ's behalf: Be reconciled to God" (2 Corinthians 5:20 NIV).

To be an ambassador for Christ, you must be bold and courageous. This comes by declaring who you are in Him over and over until you accept it as part of your identity. You must speak with authority, remain true to the faith, defend the faith, share the good news, minister to the people, and make disciples.

"Have I not commanded you? Be strong and courageous. Do not be afraid; do not be discouraged, for the Lord your God will be with you wherever you go" (Joshua 1:9 NIV).

Remember the Holy Spirit resides within our spirit to convict our soul. We must remain vigilant to what God wants us to do, our God-given purpose. People need you in their lives. People, however, are very perceptive and will be looking at your life. They may hear, but they will not listen unless they see that you are living what you preach. Part of that is presenting ourselves in manner worthy of our calling:

"Whatever happens, conduct yourselves in a manner worthy of the gospel of Christ" (Philippians 1:27 NIV).

Our service to the Lord is a lifelong journey of constantly growing and learning. God will give us the assignments we can handle, but He will also put us in positions to mature. Our job is to be prepared. I hear a lot of pastors talk about being prepared for the return of Christ. I say be prepared and execute your calling, and you will be prepared for the return of Christ. We must take time to answer the many questions of mainstream America that have a lot of conflicting information at their fingertips. There is a lot of garbage out there that you will have to contend with. This takes preparation, continuous lifelong training, and a commitment to seek out the Word of God to life's issues. It means always bouncing your opinion off the Word of God to find truth. But be careful not to be argumentative with people who hold differing views. Our job is to present truth through the love of Christ.

"But in your hearts revere Christ as Lord. Always be prepared to give an answer to everyone who asks you to give the reason for the hope that you have. But do this with gentleness and respect" (1 Peter 3:15 NIV).

Finally, know that while you are needed to share the "good news" of the gospel and you are needed to make disciples, people are suffering out there. I believe people are seeking out the Lord all the time but are wounded. Be one who will tend to their needs, and make yourself available for God to send to the harvest.

"Then he said to his disciples, "The harvest is plentiful, but the workers are few. Ask the Lord of the harvest, therefore, to send out workers into his harvest field" (Matthew 9:37–38 NIV).

Review/Application Questions

1. In what area do you feel like you are falling short on your God-given purpose or in life in general? Why do you think that is?
2. What do you think your target looks like? What do you need to do to improve your shot group and get closer to the bull's-eye?
3. What are some things you can do to prepare to share the "good news" to lead someone to Christ and not fall short?
4. Based on the reading of this chapter, did you learn anything more about the Great Commission and what you need to do?
5. What is your view on baptism, and do you think you have the authority to administer one?
6. Does your local church have a discipleship training program? If not, do you think you have what you need from this chapter to help establish one?
7. What do you think are some important things in ministry that you must remain vigilant about to mitigate the instances where you may fall short?

CHAPTER 11

NEED FOR CHAPLAINS

We cared for you. Because we loved you so much, we were delighted to share with you not only the gospel of God but our lives as well.
—1 Thessalonians 2:8 NIV

A Case for Chaplains

A CHAPLAIN IS A MEMBER of a ministry or church assigned to an institution, facility, ship, camp, base, post, and/or organization to function as a pastor to people outside the local church. A chaplain is a pastor within a health-care facility, a military organization, a law enforcement/first responder agency, or corrections facility. They are there to provide "free exercise" of religion, which is a constitutionally mandated requirement for the government. To me, a chaplain does not need to be constrained by denominational endorsement even though many are. I am a proponent of a chaplain just being a Christian who is willing to set aside theological difference to work throughout and for the body of Christ.

The case for chaplains has biblical justification. We are supposed to serve outside the church. I hear it said on numerous occasions that we go to church to worship God, to be around our church family in Christ, to be spiritually recharged, and to be equipped to serve Jesus throughout the week. Even though the word *chaplain* never appears (just like the word *trinity* never appears) in the Bible, that does not mean there is no strong biblical support for it. Hopefully, you have found this book to provide substantial support both biblically for chaplains and for the need of chaplains in secular society. Think about what is going on in our country today; the need is real. Think about what is happening in our government. There is an overwhelming need to minister in government institutions such as Capitol Hill, all the branches of the Armed Forces, police departments, fire stations, emergency services, correctional facilities (to minister to the guards), veterans' organizations, Veterans Administration hospitals, hospice facilities, and veteran assisted-living residences.

You have learned throughout this book the importance that chaplains have in working with veterans and first responders in areas of crisis and trauma. You also now know how to help those who separate from service and the inevitable effects of dealing with an identity crisis. Dr. Whit Woodard used the phrase *ministry of presence*[52] to describe chaplains ministering in an environment outside the church where others live and work in secular society. I proclaim that chaplains are assigned to a special mission by God outside the church. They must be assertive to establish relationships with those who serve but be present regularly to build rapport. They must have the "heart" for it. They address and minister to each of the four types of wounds, help people through their H3 cycle, and provide encouragement when people fall short. But they need the support of the local church, and they are a significant force multiplier for the church and their community.

I have run into so many veterans and first responders who have served who now feel "called" by God to "give back" to their brothers and sisters in their profession and to serve God. One of the best ways to do this is to become a chaplain. Everyone has their views about chaplains, especially in the military. Whether those views are positive

[52] Woodard, Whit. 2011. "Ministry of Presence: Biblical Insight on Christian Chaplaincy." North Fort Myers, Florida: Faithful Life Publishers. Faithful LifePublishers.com.

or negative, being a chaplain in your community and for your local church may be precisely what God is calling you to do. Many who have been called by God possess the skills needed. They can lead small groups, put on events, and even talk to those who have served. They come with instant relatability by their experiences and can speak their language. The difference for a chaplain is the additional training they get in taking their experiences, their skills, and their knowledge and combining it with advanced discipleship training and a refined God-given purpose. It is about the "how" to help someone in need suffering from the four types of wounds, not just being there. It is about getting them to see their God-given purpose, not just attend church. It is about helping them navigate their H3 cycles, not just encouraging them to get help. Combine that with advanced biblical training, ordination, church endorsement, an understanding of resources in your area, great mentorship, and a firm connection with the Holy Spirit, and you will be an unstoppable ambassador for Christ.

"And whatever you do, whether in word or deed, do it all in the name of the Lord Jesus, giving thanks to God the Father through him" (Colossians 3:17 NIV).

Chaplains for Churches

Churches need to commission chaplains now! I know this is a new concept to many pastors that I am sure most have not even contemplated until now. But it fills a need in every community that is not being met today. Veterans and first responders are not getting the support they need. If you want to make an impactful change, this is it! One of the most needed ministries that exist within a church is a discipleship training program. So much so that it needs to be on equal footing and equally funded as your children's ministry. I am also a huge proponent of having a military and first responder ministry in a church, second to discipleship training but inclusive of it. I would furthermore state that churches need chaplains and can assist with all these efforts.

There is not a single chaplain I license, certify, and/or endorse through our ministry who does not have the support of their pastor at their local church. This serves two purposes. First, Jesus is the head of the church, and it is the church that Jesus established. Every chaplain must be part of a local church, and their pastor must recognize both their calling and their maturity to minister to someone else. They must be in good standing with their local church. I also do not ordain a chaplain without the support of the local church pastor. I encourage churches to join me in commissioning chaplains. Second, I want the churches to know that chaplains can exist in their community and church to be able to not only support veterans and first responders in their congregation but also bring those they minister from outside organizations and encourage them to attend the church. I want the church to know they have an evangelist and someone who makes disciples out there who will bring people to the church. We need the church to support their special mission from God.

I think just about every church is missing this essential opportunity when it comes to chaplaincy. Most churches have deacons or elders to minister to people within the church, but they rely on their laity to minister to those outside the church. As we have previously stated, most people do not know how to evangelize or how to make disciples, so it mostly does not happen. There are many who are called by God, and you do not have room on your staff for all of them. But you also need people engaging the community around you. Small groups are great, but they fall short. Not suggesting you change any programs you currently have in your church, just that you join in the commissioning of chaplains. Chaplains are evangelists and discipleship makers! If commissioned and ordained, they will be even more impactful than your deacons within the church. They will strengthen the congregation throughout the week and be impact warriors for the kingdom in your community.

Recommendation. Every Christian church begins commissioning chaplains to serve in their community with a special mission. For Serve Ministries Inc., this special mission is to minister to veterans and/or first responders. We are more than willing to support you in the establishment of your program.

"Since, then, we know what it is to fear the Lord, we try to persuade others. What we are is plain to God, and I hope it is also plain to your conscience" (2 Corinthians 5:11 NIV).

Military Chaplains

"The fruit of the righteous is a tree of life, and the one who is wise saves lives" (Proverbs 11:30 NIV).

Military chaplains have been in existence since July 29, 1775, by authorization of the Continental Congress for first continental army. Every regiment of the army was assigned a chaplain. Chaplains have served in every war in American history from the War of Independence to the present day.[53] They represent all five major faiths (Protestant, Catholic, Jewish, Buddhist, and Muslim) and consist of over 120 denominations.[54] Our Christian-founded nation recognized the need for chaplains from its inception but permitted room, through our Constitution, for the freedom to exercise religion even if it was not Christian.

Our First Amendment states, "Congress shall make no law respecting an establishment of religion, or prohibiting the free exercise thereof; or abridging the freedom of speech, or of the press; or the right of the people peaceably to assemble, and to petition the Government for a redress of grievances." Our First Congress saw that our army would need chaplains to minister to those who fought our nation's wars. Often misunderstood in the debate of separation of church and state (which does not appear in the Constitution) is that government should not have any religious influence. This is further from the truth. The Constitution only prevents the government from imposing any laws restricting religion. It is very disheartening to see how much religion, and particularly Jesus Christ, is being stripped from government. Unfortunately, due to the work of the American

[53] National Museum of the United States Army. "US Army Chaplain's Corps." Retrieved from https://armyhistory.org/u-s-army-chaplain-corps on June 5, 2020.

[54] Ibid.

Civil Liberties Union (ACLU) and their attempts to remove prayer from schools, "In God We Trust" from our currency, Bibles from the courtrooms, and any Christian references from our government, there is an even more pressing need to have Christian voices in our government.

For military chaplains, they have been "handcuffed" in fully exercising their faith and allowed military regulation to impose restrictions on their faith. This is unconstitutional! It also does not meet the intent of the First Continental Congress for the establishment of chaplains. We need chaplains to boldly stand for Christ. There are chaplains from the other faiths who are free to exercise their religion, but Christian chaplains are not able to pray in the name of Jesus and exercise theirs. This is outrageous, and it is time for every Christian chaplain to pick up their cross and serve the Messiah. I see far too many military chaplains just trying to have a good military career. If this is your motive, you can serve in any other specialty in the Armed Forces as a Christian and be just as effective. If you are a Christian chaplain, you represent Christ.

At the writing of this book, Serve Ministries Inc. is in the process of becoming a Department of Defense endorsing agency. Check to see if it is established by visiting our website at ServeMinistriesInc.com. I will promise you this. We will be the first DoD endorsing agency that will be a multi-Christian faith-based endorser that will have in its charter that you must represent Jesus Christ in the performance of your duties, which includes evangelizing, making disciples, and praying in Jesus's name. This is powerful because by military regulation, you must perform your duties in accordance with your endorsing agency. We will be the first to do it, and we will fight for the freedom to serve Jesus Christ. If you believe in this and are part of another endorsing agency, you seriously need to pray about switching. For new chaplain candidates who wish to go on active duty or into the reserves, do not just go with any endorsing agency. Do not just go with your denomination endorsing agency. Evaluate them carefully and make sure they will allow you to serve in accordance with your calling.

"But you, keep your head in all situations, endure hardship, do the work of an evangelist, discharge all the duties of your ministry" (2 Timothy 4:5 NIV).

Chaplains for Veterans

One of the shocking things I realized as a Christian who retired with almost twenty-seven years of service is that when you leave the military, military chaplains are not there for you any longer. Like most, I rarely used them anyways. That is why I promote chaplains to assert themselves in ministry. Most veterans look to their local church. As you are aware by now (and you can evaluate your local church), churches are really not structured to minister to you through times of transition, nor do most of them even understand the complexity of the different wounds you are dealing with. Sure, you will find plenty of people to pray for you, and that is important. But you need help. When I looked for it, they automatically recommended a psychologist when I was going through my separation physicals. Then I was subjected to a one-hundred-question survey asking me if I wanted to kill myself. I guess I passed that, and when I retired, I had Tricare and Veterans Administration services and could ask for help. But I really did not want to talk to strangers or being overanalyzed on whether I was suicidal. I just wanted help with my transition and to hear from others who had been through it. However, others who went through it (even though it was somewhat helpful) were able to give me advice and recommendations. I had to seek them out and ask. Plus, I was still dealing (am still through my H3 cycle) with the effects from my service.

This was the recognized need impressed on me by God and the birth of our ministry. Perhaps you have the same calling. As Seminary graduate with a Master of Divinity and a Masters of Religion, all the Christian Counseling courses, and all the study of psychology and sociology, I was convinced I needed to know more about "how" to actually help someone like me. Veterans need a "brother or sister" whom they can relate to who is also a "brother or sister" in Christ. The training that God has you on right now is equipping you to be a chaplain for a veteran. Chaplains are seriously needed in the church and your community. Your leadership, your heart, your reliability, your relatability, your work ethic, your passion, and your drive are all needed.

Our community chaplains must be "plugged" into and have the support of the local church, but they also need to be connected to the military chaplains in installations near them. All military chaplains need to know who you are and are a valuable resource for transitioning veterans. Many may be receptive to conducting events on the installation where you can work together and reach those on base. Others will tell you this is their responsibility. You can remind them that when they transition, they will become your responsibility. Identifying those who are close to separating can be challenging. So here are a few suggestions to get connected:

- Schedule monthly luncheons with military chaplains to establish strong relationships.
- Participate in events they do on the installation. See if you can lead or run a portion of the event.
- Identify and establish relationships with those close to separating from service.
- Start inviting them (both service member and military chaplains) to events, Bible studies, support groups, and outreach events.
- Call yourself a chaplain and have other address you as such (if you are; you can become one through Serve Ministries Inc. if you are not already). This is important for both your identity and how others "see" you.
- Build your portfolio with a workload you can commit to. Starting out, I would say three to five veterans whom you are engaging with at least every other day even if it is a simple phone call. But you must also meet with them regularly and include them in activities and do things with them. So if you can only do one or two, then just stick to that and give everything you can to do it right.

- Try to get an opportunity to speak before every Transition Assistance Program as a representative of a service in the community, not a church. They will not allow churches to speak. But they will allow a community chaplain who has a mission to minister to transitioned veterans to speak. This is a perfect place to build contacts to minister to them, and some of them may also become chaplains. Occasionally, you may even run into a transitioning chaplain.

Hospitals are also a great place to minister to veterans. Many veterans use Tricare (~50 percent), and you can start by submitting your credentials at the local hospital as a volunteer chaplain. Hospitals cherish volunteers and will support your initiative to help veterans. Some hospitals even have professional chaplain positions you can be hired into. I even encourage volunteering if they do to start out. The hospital staff will get to know you, and it will greatly enhance your chances of being hired. This is an important ministry area. Many veterans are suffering from physical wounds, but as you know now, they most likely have compounding wounds. You can be there for them and their family. Some of their wounds may even be debilitating or terminal. That veteran and that family will need you. You may be able to establish a powerful relationship with them, and you may also be the only person representing God in their lives.

Veteran organizations are also a great place to serve as a chaplain. Some are favorable to having chaplains at more of the local level such as the Veterans of Foreign Wars, American Legion, and the Disabled American Veterans. They all appear very receptive to having a chaplain join their local chapter and minister to veterans. Make sure you establish yourself as a chaplain from the beginning, and the word will spread like wildfire, and you will have plenty of ministry work on your hands. Some of the more state-, regional-, and national-level organization may not be as receptive. One of my favorite veteran nonprofit organizations is the USO. But they do not have chaplains and were not receptive to adding them because it is not in their charter. If I ever get the opportunity to speak with their president, I will try to make that change. So you simply must ask any veterans organization, and if you can get it, commit to it.

The Veterans Administration (VA) provides medical services to ~50 percent of the other veterans who have not chosen to go primarily with Tricare or another career HMO or medical plan. The VA has full-time chaplains on their staff. Serve Ministries Inc. is an official endorsing agency for the VA. They require and offer clinical pastoral education (CPE) that will lead to National Board certification. They require a seminary degree with ministerial experience. That, with the endorsement from a VA endorsing agency, can qualify you for a full-time job as a chaplain with the VA. Serve Ministries Inc. is committed to helping those who aspire to serve in this way, and the work is imperatively needed. Of the chaplains I am aware of, most do office visitations and pray with people. We need more who understand the different types of wounds and how to minister to each.

Chaplains for Law Enforcement

Most law enforcement agencies do not have a chaplain. Some do have volunteers. Only larger agencies or departments have a paid full-time chaplain on their staff. We need to ensure that we have chaplains in every department no matter how small they are. In some cases, a chaplain can cover down on multiple small agencies. My goal is to ensure this happens in Northwest Florida. But everyone reading this book can help become an active proponent for chaplains in law enforcement. Churches need to get behind this, ministries need to push for it, and agencies need to seek it out. Law enforcement agencies/departments must make it a priority. If you care about your officers, make it happen. Chaplains are a huge force multiplier.

At the time of writing this book, we had another major incident happen in our country when Officer Derek Chauvin persistently pressed his knee on the George Floyd's neck in Minnesota that led to his death. This caused nationwide protests and a demand from the African American community for justice and reignited the "Black Lives Matter" campaign. Prejudice and injustice in America are evil acts. The action of Derek Chauvin and the failure of the other three officers on-site to protect George Floyd who was in their custody at the time he was restrained are inexcusable. The question I ask is, Where is the chaplain? According to their website, they do have a Minnesota Police Chaplain's Corps, but it is unclear how many chaplains they have.

I can tell you as the Niceville Police chaplain that this work is imperative to talk to these officers. Society will tell you it is a training problem. I disagree! Police officers spend months in a police academy and have year-round reoccurring training. This is a spiritual problem where an evil spirit took hold of Derek Chauvin in his soul where he had no respect or regard for human life. Some will say officers need Christian values. I would not necessarily disagree, but it is more than that. Police officers must have chaplains speaking into their life, offering mentorship, being a voice of sanity and encouragement, praying over them for wisdom and discernment, providing resiliency training, and speaking to officers after incidents. In the case of the Minnesota police officers, all of them had prior issues. Who was ministering to them? Who was addressing their wounds so that they would not be a danger to the community they swore to protect and defend?

Chaplains need to constantly seek training so they can also constantly inject training into the police department. As stated, training is important. We must be inserted into each officer's life and talk to them, counsel them, and pray over them. I really do not let a nonbeliever off the hook. I will still talk to them, counsel them, and pray over them. I let them feel uncomfortable about it, but I do it boldly anyways because that is my mission. I tell them up front that it is my job, so let me do it. I trust in the Holy Spirit to convict their soul. This is what we need in our country. This is one solution that can create change.

One important technique that is extraordinarily successful in connecting with law enforcement officers is to do a ride-along. I particularly like it for two reason. First, it is one-on-one time where we can both ask questions and not care about what anyone else thinks. It is safe and personal. This allows for open discussion and for both to say what is on their hearts. I find that it does not take long (sometimes in a matter of minutes) before they are sharing with me their life story and what they believe. Regardless of what I hear, it stays between us. I mostly listen and insert an occasional question for clarification. Mostly, I am assessing where they are at in life, whether they know Christ, and what potential wounds they have. I want to know about their family, their dreams, and their faith. Then I can formulate a plan to minister to them personally. Most of this happens on a ride-along too. Second, it gives me an opportunity to see their world. I never served as a police officer, so I find it fascinating to see them in action. Every officer I have been on a ride-along with has enjoyed showing me what they do. They take pride in it, and they like to share. This helps me learn more about their environment, and it builds a relationship between us. That helps me minister to them because we know each other. The hardest thing to do is to minister to someone you do not know. There is no established trust with a stranger.

Disaster planning was covered previously in chapter 6. Chaplains need to have a disaster plan to minister to the officers and their families. The department needs to be educated on your role, and you focus from the chief of police on down. We will discuss in the next and final chapter how you can get connected with your community. Even if it is a brief plan, emphasizing that you will minister to the officers and maybe their families in a time of a disaster is important. For our area in Northwest Florida, we occasionally get hurricanes and an occasional tornado warning. We are only a couple of years removed from Hurricane Michael that fortunately did not hit Niceville. We must be prepared in the event one does hit us. Our officers are already understaffed and will only be overwhelmed at storm impact.

It is best to understand all the training opportunities that exist in a department. Marksmanship training is a good place to connect and bond with officers. Resiliency training is a perfect place for you to speak. Prevention of excess use of force training is a great place to speak. Sometimes, it may seem that a training event will not be a target of opportunity to have a chaplain role, but they all do. Even if it means you are only present gives you an opportunity to insert yourself into a discussion. Remember that you are a representative of God and that you must be a "ministry of presence" to connect with them. Consider participating in the training even if it is not required. Officers enjoy seeing a chaplain go through it with them.

We will discuss resources in the next chapter as well. Your job is to recognize what is needed and what can potentially be needed in a time of crisis. However, this also includes services outside of the department. The biggest fear a police officer has is showing weakness or problems as to their chain of command that could impact their career. This is where you must have the discernment to recognize a need, meet with them one-on-one, and discuss options that the department will never know about. I have officers who get help from other ministries, churches, and community resources who are kept confidential.

How do you know if you are successful at being a chaplain? I gauge these two ways. First, what does the chief of police say about the chaplaincy program (you can see what my chaplain says on my website)? What is the view from others throughout the department? Second, do I have anyone who calls me? Does the department think to call the chaplain when something happens? Does an officer call me to talk? When these things are happening, I consider these signs of success. It is not the number of people I lead to Christ, how many classes I teach, or any other measurement that someone would define on a performance appraisal (not that I get one anyways). To me, it is whether the department comes to me with needs. It shows I am connected and that I have established trusted relationships.

"Therefore, Your Majesty, be pleased to accept my advice: Renounce your sins by doing what is right, and your wickedness by being kind to the oppressed. It may be that then your prosperity will continue" (Daniel 4:27 NIV).

Chaplains for Fire Stations/Emergency Management Services

I see many fire stations and Emergency Medical Service (EMS) or emergency management teams (EMTs) starting to merge in a single station. However, I see other EMS/EMTs becoming more privatized. For the purposes of this topic, I am combining them together because the approaches are the same. When a 911 call comes in for one of these services, it is either a false alarm or an actual crisis. On any given day, they can be responding to a traumatic event of someone else where it can be traumatic or at least a crisis for them. That is their job, but they are human. Even though they may become somewhat desensitized over time on the job, they are still being wounded.

We need chaplain coverage over every fire station and EMS station. If they are combined, that can be covered by the same chaplain. If they are separate, it can still be covered by the same chaplain. In a low-populated county, all the services of law enforcement, fire, and emergency services can be covered by the same chaplain. In larger cities, you may need an entire team of chaplains for each department/station. The idea is that everyone is covered and that each chaplain understands how to minister to personnel when they go through crisis and trauma. Combining coverage over multiple departments/agencies/stations may even open the potential for a full-time position paid for by the country, town, or city.

"That the man of God may be perfect, thoroughly furnished to all good works" (2 Timothy 3:17 NIV).

Chaplain for Corrections

I come across prison and jail ministries all the time. They all have one thing in common. They minister to the inmates. It is particularly important work and is impactful for their lives, especially when they become released. What I do not see a lot of is ministering to the guards. They must deal all day with some of the most dangerous men and women of society who have been convicted of some heinous sins. It is a dangerous work environment that contains long work hours, ever-changing shifts, and highly stressful situations. Then when their shift is up, they come out from behind the walls of the incarcerated and go home to their families.

Who is ministering and talking to them? Why does ministry after ministry just focus on the inmates? I even found that one prison had a chaplain on staff who ministered predominately to the inmates. He professed he would minister to the guards, but that was not his focus. He could not explain why and quickly realized that he needed to shift to including ministering to the guards more often. My brother, Don Renault, works as a corrections officer in Arizona and stated that chaplains ministering to the guards are almost non-existent. It is important for corrections facility wardens to recognize the need and seek adding a chaplain to minister to the guards. It is also important with those who have been called by God to serve to think about becoming a chaplain to minister to the guards rather than to the inmates. Your experience, relatability, and passion can make a significant impact in their lives. It may even be your God-given purpose.

"For this cause also thank we God without ceasing, because, when you received the word of God which you heard of us, you received it not as the word of men, but as it is in truth, the word of God, which effectually works also in you that believe" (1 Thessalonians 2:13 NIV).

Fight for the Budget

I really think highly of people who are willing to volunteer, especially in ministry. We can see God at work in their lives and their heart to make a difference for the kingdom. Unfortunately, most still must have a way to make a living. Ministry is extremely important godly work with eternal impacts. Chaplains are a force multiplier that can positively impact your organization in a phenomenal way. Just think about it, wouldn't any government organization be better off with God in it? I assure you if He is not, Satan is. But I do not approve of the notion that this is solely volunteer work that can be done by chaplains that can serve when they have time. Each of them has a real calling. It would be far more impactful if it became their full-time profession.

Now chaplains do not work for the chain of command. This is one of the issues with chaplains in the military—they work for the commander. I promote that I work for God. If the department ever becomes unhappy with my performance, if there is ever an issue with my character, or if the appointment just is not working out for whatever reason, the chief can always ask for my resignation. But my chief knows I do not work for him. I work for God through Serve Ministries Inc. I also do not get an evaluation from the chief or from anyone. I minister to them from the top down and from the bottom up. I minister to everyone on an individual basis. When I speak with the chief of police, I want to hear his heart for his officers. I want to know his concerns. I minister to him, and I never divulge information about any of his officers. He knows I refer officers to other services anonymously, and I share with him my ministry ideas for plans and training. But then I pray over him.

We need to encourage departments to have full-time paid chaplains on the payroll, even if they are on a county payroll to cover multiple departments. A professional chaplain can cover more officers and have a great embedded impact on an organization. I use the military chaplaincy model, except for working for the commander, as a baseline. Every first responder organization and veterans' organization needs professional chaplains.

However, if there is resistance to adding the chaplain to the payroll, know that it is common. There is even a belief that exists that chaplains should not be paid because they should not be doing it for money. Although this is true, I profess the notion of serving without compensation is non-biblical. There are plenty of example about the need for people to give their first fruits to those who have been called to minister for God. They are to be "set apart" to do His work. We really need to be able to focus on our God-given purpose and still have the means to provide for ourselves and our family. This has relegated most of the volunteer chaplaincy work to retirement-age Christians who have a pension. This is not a bad thing since they come with extraordinary wisdom in the faith. But it should not be so limiting with so many needs out there. It is also great to have a blend of young mature Christians where the age gap between those who serve in government and the chaplain is not so great for relatability. Either way, fight the good fight whether you are a paid professional chaplain or a volunteer. You have access, and you have authority, so serve! Promote and ask to be added to the budget, but serve regardless. Call on us to champion for you.

"Who will have all men to be saved, and to come to the knowledge of the truth" (1 Timothy 2:4 NIV).

Review/Application Questions

1. Explain why chaplains are needed in government.
2. Why is the local church important in chaplaincy?
3. What is the biggest issue for serving Christ faced by military chaplains? Is there a solution?
4. Do you think a chaplain for veterans is a good idea? Why?
5. What are the needs for chaplains in law enforcement? Do you think it can be impactful?
6. What is a way for a chaplain to cover multiple organizations in a community?
7. Is there a need for chaplains in prison/jail facilities? Why and who is mostly going unserved?

CHAPTER 12

UNITING A COMMUNITY

Whatever you do, work heartily, as for the Lord and not for men, knowing that from the Lord you will receive the inheritance as your reward. You are serving the Lord Christ.
—Colossians 3:23–24 ESV

Churches

IT IS HEARTBREAKING TO REALIZE local churches are not united in God's will. Even in the most "Bible belt" communities in our nation, the local churches are not together as "one body" under God. Your community probably has many churches, temples, and synagogues representing different denominations and even includes churches that claim no denominational affiliation. Not all of them are Christian and therefore may not be unwilling to work with Christians. The point is this, churches are not unified under God, and they are not consolidated to address significant issues that plague a community. Instead, they exist divided into sects ministering to the flocks that gravitate toward them. Many have no impact on the community at all, while others have outreach projects to give members in their congregation an opportunity to serve. Most intend to do good, but few are impactful in the community. You can probably observe and point out a couple of churches that have had impact at times. It is rare, but there are a few churches that do extraordinary work in their community. I have seen some churches do incredible things especially in times of natural disasters. Others have taken on a public need as part of their mission, such as halfway houses and planned parenting clinics. You can also probably point out far more churches, however, that you have never heard of doing anything in the community. It is an unfortunately sad realization, but many churches have no mission outside of their walls. They exist only to serve their attendees and their own institutional existence.

This is even more disturbing to me when it comes to Christian churches. I do not expect non-Christians churches to work with anyone else since they are not led by our Lord. But Christian churches are all part of the same body of Christ under the headship of Jesus. It just does not always seem like it in a community because they mostly do not work together. They have their own programs funded by their own congregation with their own objectives. There are many reasons for this, but that lack of synergetic effort to solve community issues often leaves many issues going unresolved. This exists predominately because of theological differences, interpretational disagreements, stylistic preferences, cultures, and traditions. Some church unfortunately has ulterior motives, feeling that gaining publicity in the community will lead to greater attendance and membership numbers. They may feel "they" are the solution…ideologically. But often it is about their church growth or about their survival. This gives the perception that churches are more concerned about being in competition with one another than they are about being part of the same body of Christ and caring for the people.

"I appeal to you, brothers and sisters, in the name of our Lord Jesus Christ, that all of you agree with one another in what you say and that there be no divisions among you, but that you be perfectly united in mind and thought" (1 Corinthians 1:10 NIV).

As Christians, we all know better. We all have an innate ability to be perceptive and can sense the geniality of a church. I believe the Holy Spirit gives us an increased awareness to discern how genuine a church is and whether His Spirit is present. Does the church care, or are they about getting a new building? Do they care, or are they about having nicer equipment? Do they care, or do they want more money to grow their staffs with greater benefit packages? Do they care, or is it about their pastor having a larger platform to speak from? Are they more concerned about attendance numbers, and do they care more about their membership lists? This is not to insinuate that larger or even megachurches are like this because it even exists in smaller churches. However, there is a litmus test to evaluate how a church is within your community. What do they do to make a difference in your community? What issues in the community are they committing to solving? Would the community suffer if that church closed its doors? Would the community even notice the church went away? Not just to their attendees but the community at large.

I propose a solution that Christian churches unite in the name of Jesus in their community. Imagine a community where the churches act like one body of Christ and pull together His resources to solve a community problem. Can it happen? Of course, it can. I even believe all the churches involved would even grow from it. I am not just talking financially or membership-wise; I am talking about spiritually. It is not a competition among churches. People will always want stylistic differences and want choices to find the "best fit" for their family. I think all the churches involved would grow because more people in a community will want to hear what a church has to say if they know they care. People will be willing to be a part of these churches if they see the church has a purpose in the community. People want to know churches care about them. I even think people are searching for it. Churches just need to be willing to put their theological differences aside to work with one another and focus on community needs.

"So, in Christ we, though many, form one body, and each member belongs to all the others." (Romans 12:5 NIV).

A simple solution is a ministerial association where pastors in the community meet regularly to discuss community issues. It should be a separate nonprofit organization where the pastors vote on their leadership. They should meet in a neutral location like a community center or the chamber of commerce boardroom. I recommend this because pastors usually will not agree to meet to be a part of another church's vision. They must all want to come together on equal footing. It sounds a lot like a pride issue, and it probably is, but we will be unsuccessful at fighting it. The question is, Who will take the lead to set it up? In our community, there is an association that does bring pastors together, but it is not attended by every Christian church leader even though they are all invited. It is far from a perfect example, but it has value. A pastor can present an issue, and the pastors collectively discuss solutions. Sometimes, one of the churches will take the lead on the project while other churches commit to tasks. Other times, they share in putting on an event for the community. It is often a negotiation to mitigate expectations, but it works…and it is a start.

"Be completely humble and gentle; be patient, bearing with one another in love. Make every effort to keep the unity of the Spirit through the bond of peace. There is one body and one Spirit, just as you were called to one hope when you were called; one Lord, one faith, one baptism; one God and Father of all, who is over all and through all and in all" (Ephesians 4:2–6 NIV).

For the purposes of ministering to veterans and first responders, it starts with the recognition that our community has veterans and first responders who attend each of the Christian churches in the community. Like anyone else, they based their decision where to attend on their own preferences of what they think is best for their family. Most churches honor and respect the sacrifices that they make to keep us all safe and free. However, service comes with sacrifice. Our protection of our nation and our communities comes at a cost. You have read about the costs throughout this book. The needs and the wounds are real. Unfortunately, with all the churches in the community, their needs are still going unmet because the problem is not being addressed. I think it is due to a lack of education. This is where chaplains are important. Churches do not know how to minister to a suffering veteran or a suffering first responder. Pastors are just expecting their congregations to attend church and for God to serve their needs. Therefore, *I recommend pastors start commissioning chaplains and consider having a first responder and/or military ministry in their church.* It is acceptable to combine veterans and first responders together into one ministry, but there will be aspects of that ministry that will have to be separated.

Ministries' focus areas (examples, not a complete list) include the following:

- veteran community services assistance
- Veterans Administration claims assistance
- Hospital visitations and appointment assistance
- Crisis and trauma support groups (separate military, police, and fire)
- Counseling services
- Discipleship training
- Bible studies/small groups
- Homeless Veteran intervention
- Transition assistance
- Chaplaincy development/classes
- Support to families of deployed service members

If you are reading this, chances are, God is calling on you to be a voice within your church and to serve within your community. I see the Lord moving in a significantly different way today. I see God raising up great men and women disciples from out of the ranks of our military, law enforcement, and fire stations for a special mission. I see the Lord calling on them even though many of them are struggling with how to answer the call. Many look to the church, only to find out quickly that they need to become small group leaders to help a few others who struggle with what they have also experienced. They serve the best way they can, often unequipped and untrained, but they still find ways to be impactful. But I see a far greater reformation that is about to happen. I see God raising up these men and women to prominent ministerial positions to administer to those who serve. I may be somewhat biased, but I believe those who serve are the best at serving God once they get established in His work. Due to the millions of unreached needs going unaddressed, I believe God will "rise up" those willing to answer the call, and I believe He is doing it now!

"And we urge you, brothers and sisters, warn those who are idle and disruptive, encourage the disheartened, help the weak, be patient with everyone" (1 Thessalonians 5:14 NIV).

I teach, preach, and promote the need to make disciples that can minister to those who serve to every Christian pastor, corporate leader, community leader, and ministry leader willing to listen. I brief this before the pastoral association in our community. I must get past most of them wanting to give me unsolicited advice on what they think I should. I do not mean to be facetious, but I usually get them to back down once I tell them, "Sounds great. The Lord must be really pressing that on your heart, so let's work together to do it." I do not get too many takers. I am one man trying to do what God is calling on me to do, but it takes a body of saints to make a difference in a community. I try instead to get them to take a moment to listen to the needs of our veterans and first responders. When they stop briefly to listen, I have found that they are willing to consider solutions. It is difficult work to get churches moving; most are like any organization. They are resistant to change, especially if it was not their idea. The only way I have found success is to give proof of the issues and provide solution options. Then I ask how they can help. I have learned not to expect much in return as I have been hurt by having expectations. Instead, I am an ambassador of Christ who communicates what God has placed on my heart and asks who will join in meeting the needs within our community. I work with those willing to come along and serve and not spend much energy on those not willing to be part of the solution.

Ministries

The ministries referred to in this section are nonprofit Christian organizations. Most are tied to a church and/or denomination. Others were established by Christian leaders to address needs in the community that churches were not meeting. You know about some of them. They are homeless ministries, battered women ministries, antiabortion ministries, and more. I propose a ministry for our veterans and a ministry for our first responders. In our community, it is

Serve Ministries Inc. Like any ministry, you have visions to change the world. I realistically needed to start in my backyard. Ideally, a ministry should run through a church. I feel every church should have a ministry for veterans and first responders. I even suggest that this type of ministry is so imperative in military communities that it should be equally resourced and have the same emphasis that churches place on children's ministries. There should be a pastor on staff leading it and developing enriched programs to meet needs.

"So that there should be no division in the body, but that its parts should have equal concern for each other. If one part suffers, every part suffers with it; if one part is honored, every part rejoices with it. Now you are the body of Christ, and each one of you is a part of it." (1 Corinthians 12:25–27 NIV).

Your community most likely also has several nonprofit organizations. Many of them do not have anything to do with God, but they serve an identified community need. I tend to gravitate toward those who serve God, but there is also a ministry opportunity to work with other non-Christian nonprofits. They have people willing to serve, and that gives ministers or chaplains an opportunity to express gratitude, offer prayer, and even roll up their sleeves and chip in. It is a nonthreatening way to share the love of Jesus while serving those in the community. Again, people are more receptive to hear when they see that you care. God has given me a heart to love people, so I just enjoy serving with them. If I feel led to share, I share. Results are not up to me; they are up to the Holy Spirit. It is simple to form a solid relationship with another nonprofit (even if they are secular) because both parties will have two things in common—serving a need in the community and managing limited resources. We can do so much more working together. You may be surprised, but there are most likely a lot of Christians in these secular nonprofit organizations who mobilized for the good cause when their local church did not.

Corporations

Ever since September 11, 2001, and the horrible terrorists' attacks on this nation, we have seen a significant increase in support for our veterans. Corporations stepped up and offered discounts, free services, and some even shipped supplies for free to the troops serving in Iraq and Afghanistan. I personally like Gillette razors to this day because when I deployed, Gillette always sent razors for free to the troops. Not only were they free, but they were great razors that I have since became accustomed to. Now I am a customer for life of that company because they were a supporter of me and my soldiers. I am very humbled by companies that clearly honor our veterans like this. Coming home between deployments and having a restaurant comp my tab, going into a gas station and getting a cup of coffee and the owner saying it is on him, or boarding a plane and the service agent bumping me up to first class for free were all emotional experiences. I have seen the best come out of business owners in the way they treat our veterans. I previously looked at business owners as people just wanting to make a profit, but not the real Christian and/or American ones. Usually, I forget to ask if a company offers a military discount, and my wife gets on to me about that. But when it happens, it means more to me emotionally than any money that I save.

I have seen similar gestures of kindness by corporations for police officers. As their chaplain, I go out with them on ride-alongs in the community and have seen them get free coffee from businesses. Other establishments like having police officers visit them. Perhaps it is because they feel an extra sense of security when they visit their establishment, but I also see genuine appreciation for their service. I hear many appreciation statements of "Thank you for your service" also going to police officers. This is refreshing in these days. At this writing, there are violent protests throughout the nation due to the tragic killing of George Floyd by a Minnesota police officer. Many police officers in my opinion are living "their Vietnam era" with the seemingly lack of public support for cops. But although this view is widespread, I still see individuals and companies rally to support our police officers. I see people still thanking officers. It is a great thing to see as I think 99.9 percent of all police officers serve with honor. This is not an issue I have seen with other first responders. Everyone seems to love firemen and emergency services personnel. But police officers are needed, and they need to be ministered to during these difficult times.

Corporations want to have a positive impact in the community. I think some companies want the public approval for good business. But I think many of them genuinely care about people. There is a perfect opportunity to get them involved in ministry. Outreach requires resources, and corporations want to sponsor good causes. Run a charity fundraising 10K run in your community to get service dogs for veterans suffering from anxiety and PTSD, and you will find companies willing to be a sponsor for the event. Corporations, like people, want to serve others out of the kindness of their hearts and to show gratitude. Your ministry can have greater impact by promoting your cause to corporations.

If your ministry is part of a church, then you are covered under their tax exemption status. However, stand-alone ministries need to formalize their organization as a nonprofit by becoming an IRS 501(C)(3) organization. This allows all donations (monetary, equipment, or services) to your ministry organization to be tax-deductible to the corporation. Companies will ask for a copy of your letter for their tax records. The clearer you can communicate your mission and the needs, the more likely companies will help. You want to hold a community job fair for veterans separating from the military after a service drawdown, and companies will sponsor the event and come in force with booths to represent their companies willing to interview veterans on the spot.

Community Leaders

People who service in public office are far more approachable than you think. Before I went into ministry, I do not recall ever having a conversation with a councilman, a major, a sheriff, or a chief of police. Now I seek them out to get to know them and for them to know me. Unlike common belief, you can be in ministry, and the government does not shy away from you. They are usually very respectful, and they value your position. They are also interested in what you see happening in the community. I always make it a point to discuss the needs of veterans and first responders in our community. I also tell them how our organization intends to be part of the solution and what we intend on doing. Community leaders do not know what to do with a concept. But they can support a solution.

I told community leaders that we need to train other veterans to minister to the needs of veterans suffering from the effects of their deployments. I mentioned, I believe, a trained veteran is the best way to minister to a veteran because they have instant relatability and credibility when they speak. I had several community leaders show interest, but it was a concept. I said first responders need to be trained to help other first responders, but this too was a concept. Community leaders may agree with you, but they may not know what to do with this information. So I had to develop solutions for the community.

I told community leaders and my ministry staff that we were going to hold a community social to bring corporate leaders, church leaders, and ministry leaders together to network so we can synergize our community efforts to meet veteran and first responder needs. Our plan was also to develop a community ministry directory, and they showed interest. When I said it was needed because nobody knew of all the existing services in the community, it raised eyebrows. When I said I wanted every government official, every church, every ministry, every chaplain, and every company in the chamber of commerce to have a copy for free so they could refer veterans and first responders to services, they all wanted to know how to help. I mobilized a friend who knew these community leaders to ask them to be guest speakers at the event. I wanted them to speak from the heart of the needs of veterans and first responders. We were able to get State Representative Mel Ponder to speak to overall needs in our district/county. We were able to get retired Major General Richard Comer, former Air Force Special Operations Vice Commander, to speak to veterans' needs. And we were able to get Niceville Chief of Police David Popwell to speak about police officer and first responder needs. Most of all, they supported the solution of creating community chaplains. Solutions were tangible, and people can do something with them.

"For by the grace given me I say to every one of you: Do not think of yourself more highly than you ought, but rather think of yourself with sober judgment, in accordance with the faith God has distributed to each of you. For just as each of us has one body with many members, and these members do not all have the same function, so in Christ we, though many, form one body, and each member belongs to all the others. We have different gifts, according to the grace given to each of us. If your gift is prophesying, then prophesy in accordance with your faith; if it is serving, then serve; if it is teaching, then teach; if it is to encourage, then give encouragement; if it is giving, then give generously; if it is to lead, do it diligently; if it is to show mercy, do it cheerfully" (Romans 12: 3–13 NIV).

Chief Popwell is a huge advocate for police departments to get chaplains. We were able to interview him, and that video is used to show other police departments that have never considered having a chaplain to get one. Our ministry will train them up, certify them, and ensure they meet all agency requirements. We would even play matchmaker and send them candidates based on their requirements. That shaped another solution in the community to minister to law enforcement issues. Our goal is to have a chaplain in every law enforcement department in Northwest Florida. It is a huge undertaking. We have not been able to count all the police departments in Northwest Florida yet, but we added this as a ministry objective. We have support for it from community leaders, so over time, I believe it will be a reality.

A couple of weeks ago, I was asked by our mayor what our community needed. I was having an off day, and my mind went blank. I was not expecting to be asked a question from the mayor, and I was not prepared with an answer. I missed a golden opportunity for my mayor to know what was needed for our veterans and first responders. They need chaplains ministering to their types of wounds. I am now prepared for "that" response when it comes again. I have used it on other community leaders, and I hope I get a chance to use it on the mayor again. I like using the term of ministering to their types of wounds because it incites a question if they are paying attention to me. It usually is a question like, "What does that mean?" or "What do you mean by that?" That just gives me the open invitation to tell them all about our solution. My goal is, when I am done with them, that I have their support.

Taking a Lead

For my community, I do not like the burden of having to take the lead to rally resources to meet the needs to minister to veterans and first responders. I just did not see anyone else taking a lead role to do it. I see many programs that are either mildly effective or not effective at all. Most veterans and first responders do not even know about them. Awareness is key! When I mentioned the development of a Northwest Florida ministry directory, that came about by recognizing this need.

"Two are better than one, because they have a good return for their labor: If either of them falls down, one can help the other up. But pity anyone who falls and has no one to help them up. Also, if two lie down together, they will keep warm. But how can one keep warm alone? Though one may be overpowered, two can defend themselves. A cord of three strands is not quickly broken" (Ecclesiastes 4:9–12 NIV).

Taking the lead is like herding cats. You probably remember seeing that commercial on television. It seems almost impossible as each organization (church, ministry, corporation, and government service organization) has their own agendas. People all have their own ideas. This is a major battle, but a battle worth pursuing. Form a few organizations to work together to start helping veterans, and the word will spread through the bases and the community. Provide help to police officers, and people will hear about it. It is about establishing momentum. Things may start off slow, but more will rally when they see a difference occurring. Success breeds success!

"Each of you should use whatever gift you have received to serve others, as faithful stewards of God's grace in its various forms. If anyone speaks, they should do so as one who speaks the very words of God. If anyone serves, they should do so with the strength God provides, so that in all things God may be praised through Jesus Christ.

To him be the glory and the power for ever and ever. Amen" (1 Peter 4:10–11 NIV).

I am not suggesting that you need to be that leader in the community. If someone else is doing it, join the team. If your church is doing it, get involved. There are far too few laborers for the Lord. If you become a chaplain that touches a life for Christ when they are in need, you are an amazing servant. Do not be discouraged, do not be afraid, stand boldly, speak with authority, and serve Christ. It is a spiritual war out there. I believe if you are reading this, God already called on you. My prayer is that this book was equipping for you and that you can use this to be the "salt and the light" in your community.

"Live in harmony with one another. Do not be proud but be willing to associate with people of low position. Do not be conceited" (Romans 12:16 NIV).

Review/Application Questions

1. Does your local church clearly minister to a need in the community?
2. What needs exist in your community that need the attention of the local church?
3. Does your community have a ministerial association where pastors meet to discuss the needs in the community?
4. Do you know about the ministries that exist in your community and what they are called by God to do?
5. Have you ever been to your city's chamber of commerce? If not, plan to make a visit.
6. Who are the Christian leaders of your community? Do you know them, and do they know you?
7. What is your calling, your God-given purpose? If it is to be a chaplain or a ministry leader, are you doing it? If not, what would it take? Take the next step of faith.

CONCLUSION

Therefore, go and make disciples of all nations, baptizing them in the name of the Father and of the Son and of the Holy Spirit, and teaching them to obey everything I have commanded you. And surely, I am with you always, to the very end of the age.
—Matthew 28:19–20 NIV

I WOULD LIKE TO CONGRATULATE you on taking this journey, and my prayer is that this book helped equip you to further serve in your God-given purpose. I have not fulfilled mine if this effort did not make you more of a disciple than you were. Remember you are an ambassador of Christ, and with that comes a great responsibility. You cannot do it if you do not die to self and pick up your cross. It will be demanding, and you must be willing to be transformed. If you can do that, then you will be able to be used by God to be extraordinarily impactful in people's lives, with the results being a real heavy legacy.

For serving veterans and first responders, you have learned about the H3 cycle and the four types of wounds. You have learned about the complexities of trauma and what it is like to slip into isolation and even into darkness. You learned more about how life contains crisis and, for those who serve, what it is like to have an identity crisis when they leave service. You learned about your God-given purpose. You study the inner working of who you are within your body, soul, and spirit. You know that you are your soul, and that is the ultimate *spiritual battleground*. You also now know the importance of chaplains and the needs in the community. Plus, we discussed the need for uniting a community to meet the needs of veterans and first responders.

I think you are now equipped to do His will in your life and for you to fulfill your God-given purpose. I want you to know that however long the Lord allows me to breathe oxygen, I am here for you. You can reach out to me and my staff at any time through our ministry website at ServeMinistriesInc.com. I encourage you to refer to these chapters regularly in ministry. I encourage you to allow us to be a champion for your calling. You are not alone, nor should you go on this journey alone. You must rely on God, your local church, and other Christians. I trust in the Lord that He is raising you up for a far greater mission than you and I can imagine.

It is time for you to rise and declare before the Lord. I will put you first before anything else. It is you and me. Let Your will be done. I do not want to be what I have always been; I want you to transform me into what you want me to be. I do not want to live another day for me; I want to live for you. This is my choice to serve you, understanding that you gave me the free will to choose. I will pick up my cross so I can be a true disciple and follow you. I know this is what you want me to do. I accept the mission. Thank you, oh Lord, for calling on me—"Here am I, send me" (Isaiah 6:8 NIV).

May God bless you on your life's journey and give you strength to weather the storms. Go now and speak boldly, proclaiming the "good news" of Jesus evangelizing to the unsaved and make disciples of them as the Great Commission commands, "Be strong and courageous" (Joshua 1:9 NIV). Know that Jesus is with you every step along the way. All you need to do now is to take the next step of faith…so…*go*!

"Therefore, my dear brothers and sisters, stand firm. Let nothing move you. Always give yourselves fully to the work of the Lord, because you know that your labor in the Lord is not in vain" (1 Corinthians 15:58 NIV).

ABOUT THE AUTHOR

MICHAEL BELTON IS A FORMER Army officer who was forcibly retired after almost twenty-seven years of service as a 100 percent disabled veteran. He started off his career as an infantryman, raising to become a Sentinel at the Tomb of the Unknown Soldier during his first enlistment. He returned to the Army as an officer after going to college. He commanded in the 3rd Infantry Division during the initial Invasion in Iraq in 2003. He had served in multiple deployments to Iraq and Afghanistan, who experienced firsthand the impacts of crisis and trauma both personally and to the soldiers around him. Now being called by God to minister to those who serve or have served, he formed a multi-Christian faith nonprofit organization called Serve Ministries Inc. where he is the president and lead chaplain that ministers to veterans and first responders in Northwest Florida. He is also currently serving as the Niceville Police Department chaplain. Michael graduated from seminary at Liberty University with a Master of Divinity and a Master of Religion. He also has a Master of Aeronautical science from Embry-Riddle Aeronautical University and a BS in Public Administration from James Madison University. He has been serving in ministry for over twelve years, now primarily focused on veterans and first responders suffering from the experiences of their service. He is a passionate advocate for community chaplains, speaking to community leaders about having chaplains for every first responder department/agency, talking to pastors about the need of military and first responder ministries in all Christian churches and the importance of every church having a discipleship training program. Michael strongly believes people are not reaching their full potential in serving God. His hope is that you find this book equipping as a disciple and inspiring to fulfill your mission, your God-given purpose.

Printed in the USA
CPSIA information can be obtained
at www.ICGtesting.com
LVHW070924271023
761953LV00020B/36/J